The
FRENCH
ROOM

The
French
Room

Betty Lou Phillips, ASID

Photography by Dan Piassick

GIBBS SMITH
TO ENRICH AND INSPIRE HUMANKIND

Salt Lake City | Charleston | Santa Fe | Santa Barbara

First Edition
12 11 10 09 08   5 4 3 2 1
Text © 2008 by Betty Lou Phillips
Photographs © 2008 by Dan Piassick

Published by
Gibbs Smith
P.O. Box 667
Layton, Utah 84041

Orders: 1.800.835.4993
www.gibbs-smith.com

Designed by Cherie Hanson
Printed and bound in China
Gibbs Smith books are printed on either recycled, 100% post consumer waste, or FSC certified papers.

Library of Congress Cataloging-in-Publication Data

Phillips, Betty Lou.
   The French room / Betty Lou Phillips ; photographs by Dan Piassick. — 1st ed.
      p. cm.
   ISBN-13: 978-1-4236-0455-6
   ISBN-10: 1-4236-0455-5
   1. Interior decoration—United States—History—21st century. 2. Decoration and ornament—France—Influence. I. Piassick, Dan. II. Title.
   NK2004.15.P56 2008
   747.0944—dc22
                              2008016109

FRONT JACKET: *Taking inspiration from the shapely, gracefully displayed containers holding colored water in the lobby of Paris's grand Hôtel Crillon gives rise to a sophisticated greeting room where an array of textures adds character and a bronze-and-taupe palette helps visually enlarge the space. The table with a reflective finish is from Murray's Iron Works, Los Angeles. Reveling in its glow are chairs in the style of Louis XVI by Nancy Corzine. A decidedly French bar cart—from KM Antiques, New York—takes the place of the usual table. The "Versailles" sofa is from the Cameron Collection, Dallas. The nineteenth-century limestone fireplace is from France.*

BACK JACKET: *In the midst of summer, chairs from Murray's Iron Works—dressed in cocktail recipes hand painted by Houston artist Allan Rodewald—make a fashion statement that's sure to turn heads.*

END PAPERS: *"Constantino" from prestigious Christopher Hyland swathes châteaux, villas and palazzi worldwide and the end pages of* The French Room.

TITLE PAGE: *Besotted as we are with France's architecture and landscaping—not to mention the French art of living—we glean inspiration for a rich array of estates across the United States reflecting historical precedents but with modern conveniences, of course. Delighting the eye and satisfying the spirit is this Dallas residence designed by Clint Pearson. Tatum Brown Custom Homes brought enduring quality to the construction. And indeed worthy of the French monarchy is the landscaping, by Harold Leidner Company.*

OPPOSITE: *Understated elegance reigns in an entry with ample historical references. The painted settee, a marquise (a wide, low-back bergère capable of accommodating two people that became the prototype for the loveseat) and marble table are all old, the latter unearthed at Kay O'Toole Antiques in Houston. The leopard runner is from Stark Carpet. In seventeenth-century French châteaux, staircases swept to the right—ensuring that right-handed men defending the estate from the top of the stairs could comfortably swing their swords to the right. Testaments to this architectural ideal continue today.*

CONTENTS

In the orderly world of the French, most everything must be within easy reach. And while large cracks are not especially desirable in pots de confit—which once preserved duck or goose for cassoulet, a South of France specialty—most stateside collectors expect to see signs of wear.

ACKNOWLEDGMENTS

To simply say "thank you" hardly seems adequate, but I would like to warmly thank the many people who helped air-lift The French Room *and its 200 images to press. For without their help, this book would not be.*

Special thanks, therefore, goes to those who opened the doors to their splendid châteaux and permitted us to photograph their residences: Heather and Bill Esping, Lisa and David Faulkner, Ruth and Jack Gay, Francie Faudree Gillman and Dale Gillman, Staci and Jeff Mankoff, Marsha and Bill Rickett, Lisa and Jay Ryan, Chris and George Tamke, Radonna and John Vollmer, Cathy and Jeff Wood and more.

I appreciate, too, the distinctive way of defining style—with a chic blend of the traditional and edgy—of the following designers: Laura Lee Clark Falconer, Sydney Fiedler, Francie Faudree Gillman and Dale Gillman, Sarah Lander Hast, Richard Gordon, Bill Hendrix, Pam Pierce, Carol Ray and Marlene Weitman, Lisa Luby Ryan and Liz Lank Williamson.

Also, I am personally grateful to those who worked overtime so our own projects could become an integral part of this book: Price Avent, Susan Brown, Donna Burley, Nancy Caperton, Buffy Cornell, Mark Danuser, James Davis, Esther Gandal, Lupe Hayes, Jennifer Howell, Bill Lawrence, Harold Leidner, Jesus Marroquin, Shaun Christopher Marshall, Carl McGowan, Philip Minton, Jodie Newby, Jim Palmer, Allan Rodewald, Corinthia Runge, Julia Rider, Jimmy Saunders, Clair Story and Linda Swain. Thanks also go to Jennifer Chapman, Julia Foster, Christy Gatchell, Angela Malone, Gillian Bradshaw Smith, Clair Storey, Jayne Taylor, Doreen Wallace and Julie Willenbrock.

For her prized design assistance, I thank Andrea Smith time and again. Together we thank our design-savvy team: Julie Macatee, Brenda Lyle, Katie Lang and Janice Stuerzl.

Add to the above list a love and appreciation for photographer Dan Piassick, book designer extraordinaire Cherie Hanson, and my longtime editor Madge Baird— each helped polish *The French Room* to a gleam.

A comfortable haven works not only for entertaining friends but also for everyday life, thanks to a cozy palette and a mix of old and new—giving the impression that furnishings were gathered over time.

INTRODUCTION

"The real voyage of discovery consists not in seeking new landscapes, but in having new eyes."

—*Marcel Proust*

Given their strong sense of self, commanding flair and ardor for collecting, to say nothing of their *savoir-faire,* the French simply do not understand American dependence on decorators, which they view as leaving one vulnerable to uncertain results.

It's not that none would ever dream of collaborating with a design professional, only that most would never turn over control of a project even to the most capable hands. Never mind that ancestral furniture and *objets d'art* conspire to make seeking expert help unnecessary. Most see decorating as an aesthetic undertaking en route to self-satisfaction.

So, what if faced with myriad issues that warrant assistance? In that case, the French are likely to have a comprehensive plan, opt to be hands-on and be precise in requests—specifying styles, shapes and proportions in such detail that leaves little doubt about their wishes and suggests the confidence they have in their own good taste. Further ensuring the results are in keeping with the preciseness of their visions, many continue buying what they admire, upholding the exacting standards they insist upon. While adding to a trove of distinctive-looking family pieces, like-minded style setters paint flattering self-portraits revealing their creativity, interests and national pride—which is, of course, their intention.

Without fail, settings start with furnishings handed down from one generation to the next. As rooms take shape, they gather even more accoutrements that are meaningful. Determined to prevent their heritage from fleeing to far-flung cities outside France as much as striving to make stylish statements, *habitués* flock to the Hôtel Drouot, in Paris's ninth *arrondissement*, or district, where more than 2,000 auctions held annually teem with temptations for every predilection.

Until the time of Louis XVI, dining tables were uncommon. Now an appreciation for the old, the unusual, the unexpected and the unique ultimately leads to an artfully fashioned dining room that brims with culture and charm. Lee Jofa fabric covers chairs from Therien Studio Workshops, San Francisco.

In addition they spend weekends relentlessly combing the famed Marché aux Puces de Saint-Ouen, the vast flea market in existence since 1886 on the outskirts of the capital, unless scouring *les puces* (flea markets) at Vanves and Montreuil or traipsing to L'Isle-sur-la-Sorgue, the Lubéron's matchless center for antiques, with more than 250 *brocanteurs* (dealers in second-hand goods).

Even so, most interiors are neither cluttered nor intimidating. Despite the grandeur in which Louis XIV (1643–1715) and his descendants Louis XV (1715-74) and Louis XVI (1774–93) lived in the ostentatious Château de Versailles—with its approximately 700 rooms and 2,000 windows—understated beauty is a design dictum. The French equate elegance with restraint, shunning the wanton excess identified with the ousted *ancien régime*.

Ongoing sympathies to the principles that led to the storming of the Bastille prison on July 14, 1789, and overthrow of a monarchy born in 987 cut across regions and class lines in this nation of more than 60 million people. Unlike in the United States, where there is more than a hint of elitism as even in an uncertain economy a record number of men and women are making fortunes and reveling in spending them on everything

Inviting admiration, Richard Ginori layers "Fiesole," manufactured in Italy.

from high-performance cars to higher-performance airplanes to posh vacation homes in enclaves such as Aspen and the Hamptons, image-conscious Gaullists are wary of splurging on anything that might telegraph wealth. Rather, people of all economic levels link well-being with *"liberté, égalité, et fraternité!"*—the national mantra born at the onset of the French Revolution and heralded ever since.

Not that *appartements* in the Île-de-France—the very heart of France, including Paris and the seven surrounding *départements*—are devoid of glamour. Or that some do not emit an air of sumptuousness. Nearly twelve million people live in this historic region. And, by some estimates, fewer than 25 percent dwell in single-family homes.

As it turns out, most quarters are modest in size, by American standards, in spite of lofty ceilings, deeply chiseled *moulures* (moldings), patterned wood floors and untold presence. The older the building, in general, the more prestigious it is, with eighteenth- and nineteenth-century *hôtels particuliers* (family mansions now divided into *appartements*) the most adulated of all privately owned domains.

There are, of course, exceptions. But in the capital's most coveted *arrondissements*, nearly all are handed down from generation to generation rather than sold, creating an aura of exclusivity that suggests an occupant's admission into Paris's modern-day aristocracy even if not intended. Undeniably, an address alone conveys privilege to those in the know. For the French are well schooled in the art of discretion to avoid exacerbating age-old social tensions. As children they learn that talking publicly about family wealth or anything else that might stir envy or resentment is not simply taboo but by its very nature a very un-French thing to do.

Amid the intimacy that classically proportioned rooms afford unabashedly swirl shimmering taffetas, sophisticated jacquards, smart damasks and chic chairs from the beguiling Rococo period (1730–60), when Louis XV and his renowned mistress, Madame de Pompadour, had great influence on the decorative arts.

And inside the apartments, there is most certainly nothing conservative about the requisite centuries-old mirrors, valued Aubusson carpets and stone busts that sit on top of commodes carved in the era of Louis XVI, even if clean-lined neoclassicism developed as a reaction against the perceived excesses of rococo style—about which there is no doubt.

Mixing pieces from disparate periods is common practice, offering a rich lesson in art history while easing formality. But a dash of leopard fabric may also tame the seriousness of a space by making the glamorous appear more relaxed, or vice versa. Certainly, looks vary widely. Seldom do the French stray from their unified approach to decorating, however.

(Never mind that in the interest of equality, the Fifth Republic ideal ignores religious and ethnic differences so those with residency papers exude a collective identity regardless of their origins. Or that officially, all citizens are French, neatly grouped, regardless if they share or distance themselves from Gallic values.)

Those with pro-Gallic sentiments make no secret of their love for family, affection for pets and fervor for France, whether furnishing an *appartement* with a Paris address, a *château* in the Loire Valley or a *bastide* just outside the village of St-Rémy-de-Provence. But the old-world élan of their rooms may well owe even more to unspoken revelations equally instinctive that stretch back to the Sun King's haute obsession for detail and finely crafted furnishings rather than to his lavish lifestyle and glitzy fêtes.

With the wisdom gleaned from fervent beliefs that have long defined French decorating, savvy Americans—designers and not—ardently sculpt satisfying rooms that distinctly reflect individual sensibilities and stateside lifestyles yet owe more than a little to inspirations from abroad. No matter that living on this side of the Atlantic means we aren't necessarily charmed by an antique vase with a chunk missing, aren't drawn to a thread-bare carpet and may refuse to exalt the beauty of a tattered chair; we trust that the French would approve. How could they not? How indeed! For we offer an updated take on old-world artistry—fashioning spaces as different as they are dazzling—that says much about our attitudes, values and a people whose *joie de vivre* (art of living) has earned our admiration and respect.

Betty Lou Phillips, ASID

P.S. This isn't to imply that a lot can't happen in the translation when ideas and furnishings are transferred from one culture to another. With imitation now decidedly last century, being American means having the freedom to express our individual taste and confidently putting our own artistic spin on French style, whether relaxed or refined.

Les
Couleurs
De
France

LES COULEURS DE FRANCE

Taking a cue from the land, the sun and the glistening Mediterranean Sea, not from established trend forecasters, interiors echo the splendor of France the way Mother Nature intended, proponents say.

Blue—a color once believed to keep all manner of misfortune away—lands in a wave of favorite shades, from the sapphire blue that bathes the sweeping coastline to the sky blue in the cloudless countryside to the violet blue of lavender beds faded by the sun. Splashes of balmy yellow, poppy red and deeper claret shore up sites flooded with light, winning admiration, too.

Color also makes its way from faithfully tended vineyards, olive groves and wheat fields, as well as orchards with the latest crops of peaches and plums. As if that weren't enough, the shifting tones of leafy green offer even more decorating choices.

Finally, in a country entrenched in its fabled past, mellow old-world shades of ochre—whose pigments range from oxblood with undertones of brown to pale yellow—are coaxed from the earth into rooms where they vie for the right to have their say. Not that the color is limited to interiors—hardly. Seventeen painterly shades—including sienna, umber, and, not least, terra-cotta—swathe houses in the Lubéron village of Roussillon, whose rolling hills are an important resource for ochre sold around the globe.

While the color wheel is a universal tool considered helpful in pairing hues, the French maintain that world authorities cannot improve on nature, whose endless color possibilities coexist in harmony. As proof, they offer a chic mix of visual interest and drama, straying beyond conventional combinations to distinctive, unexpected choices appropriate for the room's ever-changing natural light. > 23

New or old, there's no mistaking that copper is a staple in French kitchens, mostly because it heats quickly and evenly at low temperatures and then cools quickly.

PRECEDING OVERLEAF: *A culturally rich dining room plays host to meals both fancy and less formal with Louis XV walnut commodes dating back to the eighteenth century, an Italian tiered crystal chandelier a century younger and an oil painting by Edzard Dietz, who received his formal training in Germany before settling in France. All but the latter are from Jacqueline Adams Antiques, Atlanta, and fittingly, not about to be overshadowed by the grouping of etched vessels anymore than Shaun Christopher Designs' stunning stenciled walls (repeating the Mulberry motif from chair fronts) or the Hinson & Company window treatments fabricated by Donna Burley at Straight Stitch, Dallas. Sconces (unseen) add to the ambiance during an ongoing search for an area rug.*

Most Parisians begin the day with a freshly baked croissant at their favorite boulangerie, while people in this country are more apt to perch at a breakfast bar in their own homes. The order of the day: a sampling of Vietri's "Incanto," handcrafted in Italy. The durable weave of a Bergamo fabric makes it an ideal choice for covering bar stools from Michael Shannon Associates.

OPPOSITE: A painted cupboard from Country French Interiors, Dallas, brings a rural accent to a sophisticated home. Behind closed doors is a flat-screen television mounted on an articulating bracket that allows viewing from anywhere in the breakfast room. Old walnut planks make up the table from The Old Timber Table Company, Dallas.

No matter that French chemist Michel Eugène Chevreul's pioneering work as director of Gobelins, the most important tapestry and carpeting manufacturer of the seventeenth and eighteenth centuries, contributed to the development of the color wheel. In a country that has always been defined by its regional differences—given that France's climate and terrain vary wildly—most people prefer trusting their instincts, drawing color from nature's schemes or the façades of historic sites.

Intense, saturated Mediterranean hues that can hold their own in the glaring sun fill dwellings in the South of France, where subdued tones can look lifeless and dull. By contrast, vibrant colors appear garish in Paris, which sits at about the same latitude as Seattle and Vancouver, and where a dressier spirit pervades.

In the French capital—along with other places with moody weather—posh muted shades such as oatmeal, parchment, putty and taupe project sophisticated, gracious airs that are anything but drab. Mixing subtle values of the same color appeals to the uptown sensibilities of Parisians, whose cosmopolitan style requires that fabrics and wall finishes simply complement each other rather than court attention.

Prompted by the pull of the past, some scrape centuries of paint off walls, trying to unearth the original color, or at least a layer suggestive of what once was. Dozens more see no need to make any changes to a place filled with memories that separate them from everyone else. Unlike in the States these days, where it is commonly estimated that families move every five years and then in new locales embark on campaigns to craft distinctive looks, most dwellings remain in the same family for generations—and the French tout their deeply personal histories as a way to distinguish themselves from others, sharing as a backdrop the palette of France.

Warm, glazed finishes create the illusion of age, while a collection of antique French pharmacy jars furnish vintage charm. Curtain fabric is from Cowtan & Tout.

PRECEDING OVERLEAF: Once, the kitchens in most châteaux were servants' domains, hidden behind swinging doors on the ground floor, far from the dining room to avoid scattering fires and intrusive sounds and aromas—in short, places most would seldom go. Quite the opposite, today's open kitchen has become the new greeting room, an all-purpose space that rivals a Parisian café.

OVERLEAF A late-eighteenth-century canvas that once lined the walls of a salle a manger (dining room) in a bastide (villa) in the Dordogne region of France now adds warmth and a layer of luxury to the far wall of this great room. Embracing the painting's icy blue color, nineteenth-century children's chairs, impeccably dressed in a subtle Sanderson check, cuddle up to a Hamilton coffee table. Quiet shades of gold, ivory and taupe harmoniously imbue the space with texture without pattern overload. The St. Francis bergère chairs are from the Cameron Collection, as is the down-filled sofa.

The Power of Color

Translated, an old French proverb proclaims, "A white wall is the fool's paper," not considering the thousands of paint chips now on the market that people might be left obsessing over—actually, enough to make some stick with white, despite having to deal with its numerous undertones: pink, peach, yellow, green, blue, gray, taupe and mushroom, to name just eight.

The adage does deserve credit, however, for publicizing the power of color, which can make authoritative statements, alter outlooks and help shrug off stress. It also can solve some irksome design problems—without moving walls, raising roofs, adding on or making other structural improvements, which, in this world of uncertainty, is equally impressive.

It is a stretch to say, though, that any adage would ever hold the French hostage. Those who don't subscribe to its view are quick to point out that in white lies a spectrum of colors. And that, depending on the time of day and season of the year, a room may appear gray at one hour and perhaps green another. But even they readily acknowledge that to increase the sense of space, highlight admirable architecture and quell ceiling shortcomings, it is worth adopting the following time-tested guidelines that make a room not only more alluring but eminently livable:

- Light, less-than-intense cool colors—for instance, blue and green—visually expand small quarters, prompting walls to recede so spaces appear larger than they actually are.

- Dark, warm colors—red, orange and yellow—do just the opposite. Advancing hues work overtime to make generously sized rooms appear more intimate by absorbing light.

❧ Rich, sun-drenched colors look best after dark, lit by candles, picture lights, wall sconces and carefully placed table and floor lamps—with dimmer switches adjusting lighting levels. During the day, deep colors accentuate cracks and patches on walls, plus make ceiling imperfections difficult to ignore.

❧ Tempting as they may be, riotous, sizzling hues are worth thinking twice about should the whim strike—unless living in a light-flooded region that blatantly demands colors as brilliant as the sun.

❧ Walls and molding with minimum contrast—meaning the latter are painted just slightly deeper than the former—fashionably disguise so-so trim and other surfaces lacking architectural panache, such as radiators. Avoiding visual rivalry, in turn, brings the illusion of height to a low-ceilinged room.

❧ Some argue, knowingly, that adding one-third to one-half wall color to white perceptibly elevates a ceiling to greater heights.

❧ Conversely, a ceiling painted the same color as the walls seemingly lowers the ceiling. So, too, does painting it darker than the walls.

❧ In spaces with sufficient light, a shade of white works well as a frame for contrasting walls.

❧ Garrets are not places to experiment with bold, eye-popping colors, even when bathed in light. The same serene shade on walls and ceiling masks odd contours, increases the feeling of space, and leaves a room feeling tranquil, which is indeed the goal. Enveloping walls and sloping ceilings in a small-scale-patterned paper— one that matches the mood of the times—also creates an air of spaciousness.

Day or night, a pair of nineteenth-century chandeliers—scaled to lofty proportions—stakes claim to the air space, defining multiple conversation areas.

To approximate the diameter of chandelier needed for a space, measure the width of the room in feet, double the number and convert it to inches. Another option: measure the width of the room in feet and then the length of the room in feet. Add the two, and then convert the feet to inches. An important aside: the wiring of a fixture—antique or not—should be checked before hanging, making sure it is UL approved. UL (Underwriters Laboratories) is the trusted source for product compliance, relied upon to test for safety.

OPPOSITE: An eighteenth-century armoire from Jacqueline Adams Antiques, Atlanta, pays homage to France with its importance. What most distinguishes it? Palatial proportions, deep, intricate carving, piercing, a shaped bonnet (curved top), and, indeed, the patina of time.

An authentically French Sanderson toiles de Jouy print swathes chair fronts and seats, while a Rogers & Goffigon woven cloaks backs of seating from the Renaissance Collection, Dallas. Bridge table is by Panache.

OPPOSITE: *Mixing elegance with ease warms an amply proportioned great room that works for enjoying the company of friends, playing games with grandchildren and watching television. Bolts of Nobilis and Randolph & Hein fabrics cover back-to-back sofas from the Cameron Collection, separated by an antique table—quite unlike the usual arrangement of facing sofas on either side of a fireplace. Lamps are from Nancy Corzine; shades are by Ceil Johnson, Dallas. The limestone fireplace with a commanding presence is from France.*

Gold-embroidered bumblebees embellish white linen guest towels. To break with the customs, tastes and furnishings of the ancien régime, who had chosen the fleur-de-lis as France's heraldic symbol of unity and harmony, Emperor Napoléon Bonaparte selected the bee as a symbol, seeing it as emblematic of immortality and resurrection, as had France's early sovereigns. Within hours of his coronation, Napoléon also ordered that an eagle be perched at the top of the shaft of each flag in his army.

OPPOSITE: With a separate area for sleeping and retreating, a sitting room exudes the ambiance of a posh hotel. Parisian Jeanne-Françoise Julie Adélaïde Bernard Récamier (1777–1849), a literary and political leader in the early nineteenth century, inspired the récamier—a gracefully curved daybed with one end slightly higher than the other. A portrait of Madame Récamier by French painter Jacques-Louis David hangs in the Louvre, the world's most visited art gallery.

As in most powder rooms tucked into an entry, space is tight. But limitations or not, a powder room can clearly make an elegant statement when Sherle Wagner's luxurious gold-plated fittings and brown onyx sink take center stage. (Key is having the door open outward.) The paisley tone-on-tone wall covering is from Cole & Son; the antique mirror, sconces and crystal chandelier (unseen) reflect the glamour of bygone eras.

A nineteenth-century duchesse brisée—literally "broken duchess"—infuses a master bedroom with a sense of history. Nestled together are a hand-carved Louis XV bergère chair and a low bergère-like foot piece, or ottoman, that offer a reading spot in the master bedroom. The pole lamp is from Vaughan, and the two-tiered French bar cart is from KM Antiques, New York. Fabrics from Christopher Hyland dress both the chair and the window.

OPPOSITE: *Multicultural influences, luxurious textiles and glowing wall finishes complement a palette of platinum and gold, which includes a hint of amethyst, thanks to the Murano glass lamps and the tulips. The bed is from Patina, hand painted in Italy. The nineteenth-century secrétaire and table are French. The oil painting is by Raymond Thibésart (1874–1968), a silver medalist in 1922 at the Salon des Artistes Française in Paris.*

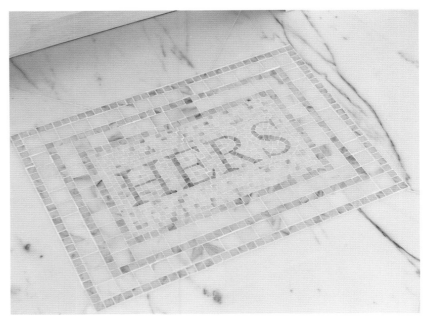

With the distinctive, uncluttered look of a European hotel, his side of the bathroom exudes cool efficiency. Fixtures are polished nickel.

UPPER RIGHT: A discreet bit of bling adds an elegant touch to a vanity stool with tufted seat and button back.

LOWER RIGHT: Her side flaunts an inlaid polished marble rug by Waterworks that is identical to his. Lettering is polished Carrara; the border is polished Calacatta gold.

OPPOSITE: To improve well-being in this stressful age, we long for our bathrooms to offer Zen-like serenity and healing properties. While calming the mind, soothing the senses and befriending the spirit in satisfying doses. Waterworks' freestanding "Candide" cast-iron tub also bathes this master bathroom in luxury. Waterworks' 18-x-18-inch polished Calacatta gold marble relaxes on floors. Highlighting walls are polished 12-x-12-inch squares——cut into pieces 6 x 12 inches then framed in marble at the top and base. Patterned towels are from D. Porthault.

Appreciation for Texture

It is hard to dispute that a room with few textures produces the feeling of space. But considering that a setting with all sleek finishes is unavoidably cold, the French find a fluid blend far more pleasing. In their minds, mixing diverse surfaces helps soothe the way to the feeling of well-being by softening hard edges and adding warmth.

As it happens, texture has a reputation for shaping rooms as much as color, whose opposites attract. Yet, integrating disparate materials can challenge even the French, mostly because layering furniture, fabrics, and lighting requires pulling together more than myriad variations of rough and smooth. Unless surfaces are both a contrast and a complement, a setting can be off-putting, even horribly jarring.

In rooms awash in the signature extremes—light and heavy, hard and soft, coarse and shiny, refined and relaxed—harmony is the ultimate goal. Whether expressing passion for timeworn furnishings from the era of the *ancien régime* or a taste for

Hand-painted tile liners on the backsplash, custom from Waterworks, add flavor in the kitchen opposite.

OPPOSITE: *With proper planning, even a small kitchen can sizzle. Adding zest to one designed for catering: a Franke sink, a Kohler "ProMaster" faucet and Pantone chili pepper—the global authority's deep, spicy red chosen 2007 color of the year. The linen Roman shade is Mulberry's "Parisian Scene."*

Highly protective of its vineyards, France has ordinances prohibiting foreign buyers from purchasing these properties without government approval, which lately has been less difficult to get. And though France continues to be the world leader in fine wines, the number of tasting rooms in the United States is growing, following reports that red wine helps prevent heart attacks.

OPPOSITE: *Appropriately, praiseworthy wines are the foundation of an artistically engineered tasting room, where offerings are written on a chalkboard, in keeping with Parisian tradition. Embossed leather chairs surround the walnut table dating back to the nineteenth century. The floor is reclaimed brick, adding years to new construction.*

Napoléon III and Empress Eugénie's Second Empire (1852–70, between the Second Republic and the Third) eclectic, overstuffed splendor, French artistry demands juxtaposing soft, sensuous surfaces among those perceived severe—the more subtly, the better.

Here's how the French do just that and then some with amazing self-assurance:

❧ Faithful to their heritage, exquisitely fashioned, hand-forged railings wrap balconies and staircases, which is hardly surprising given that the French gift for making magnificent objects from iron is well known.

❧ Unassuming fireplaces, worn wood floors—often laid in a herringbone, chevron or *parquet de Versailles* pattern—and handsome, heavy doors clad in original fittings work together, anchoring settings unpretentiously.

❧ In rooms with high ceilings, exposed wood beams fuse the

warmth and earthy charm of rural France with the unmistakably urbane sensibilities of Paris, conveying the feeling of a country house far from the capital.

❧ Glazing lends an old-world aura to textured, hand-plastered walls by reflecting light differently from paint, depending on the base and top coats used. White walls layered laboriously in translucent biscuit, for instance, give the appearance of worn parchment. (To enhance nondescript walls, American Clay Plaster in Albuquerque, New Mexico, offers a formula easily mixed with water and troweled over most any primed surface, including textured ceilings and old paint. Twelve standard colors imitate rough Provençal plaster or Venetian plaster, another decorative finish favorite.)

❧ Venetian plaster borrows alluring tints such as dove, ivory and champagne from luminous eighteenth-century silks, bestowing character.

Much has changed since the nineteenth century, when the cocktail came into its own and ornamentation became the rage as hosts strived to dazzle their guests by draping drinks with fresh fruit. Now, cool recipes give chair backs and seat cushions a distinctive spin, while skirts provide glamorous cover for once-bare legs (see back cover for the latter.) Equally important, palm-leaf place mats and banana-leaf plates—from France—make a spur-of-the-moment gathering look as if it had been planned for days. On the menu: tuna salad and fresh fruit with poppy seed dressing.

OPPOSITE: *Designed for easy living, a loggia is furnished and accessorized much like any room inside the house. But here, weather-resistant fabrics from Perennials ("Chocolate Kiss") and Lulu DK ("Fruit Punch") stand up to the sun, while French doors facilitate coming and going.*

Embroidered letters give posh towels an edge.

OPPOSITE: *A porcelain pedestal sink flanked by a Waterworks grooming bar makes it easy to put oneself back together after swimming.*

❦ Marmorino plaster (ground marble applied in layers and then buffed to a shine) also dates back to the eighteenth century. Though it is even more complicated to reproduce than it sounds, in the hands of skilled professionals the result is rewarding.

❦ Since dramatic textures attract more than their fair share of attention, Parisians use them sparingly, perhaps offering a clue why today more people favor painted rather than splashy gilded furniture. Or why area rugs are more popular than carpeting running wall to wall.

❦ Domestic furnishings are the norm. But a widely held attraction for hand-painted Italian country desks and commodes makes both increasingly difficult to find.

❦ Reflective surfaces—crystal chandeliers, antique gilt-edged mirrors and French forties coffee tables among them—multiply the light and city views, signaling a > 48

Peak vacation season or not, bright, playful colors can hold their own in the glaring sun, much like in the South of France. On deck: towels and tableware from Target and water hyacinth bolsters and floor cushions from San Francisco–based West Elm.

OPPOSITE: *Considering the negative press the airline industry has been getting lately——fewer seats, higher airfares——the ultimate retreat might be one's own milieu. Besides, with European-inspired market umbrellas from Santa Barbara Designs offering a respite from the sun, family-friendly furnishings from Murray's Iron Works and splashy fabrics sprawling across chaises, the site could be mistaken for a posh resort that's difficult to leave.*

shift in attitudes. After being shunned for most of the twentieth century, mainly due to harbored memories of war and the German occupation of France (1940–44), furnishings from the 1940s have become an increasingly popular way to add shine, prompting the French firm Pierre Frey to introduce a forties-inspired fabric collection. Noticeably, too, mercury lamps and *verre églomisé* vases (painted on the reverse side of the glass) help radiate fresh modernity.

- Cut velvets make an impressive statement, defining what it means to be fashionable without being overly bold.

- Sumptuous silk-taffeta curtains—or window treatments in other fabrics with a glossy finish—catch available light, communicating an elegant, uptown spirit that complements deep moldings and regally carved *boiserie* (seventeenth- and eighteenth-century wood paneling) glazed light gray, gray-green or gray-blue.

- Posh fabrics—some from the grand house of Braquenié—also rise to the occasion, tempering the stuffiness of oak-paneled boiserie and parquet floors, while casting in new light antique urns turned into lamps that are adorned in a gamut of stylish shades.

- Nubby weaves such as chenille, corduroy, twill, tweed and wool cast shadows that absorb light, much like advancing hues. Although warm and welcoming, they appear casual, regardless of the colorway.

- Relaxed linens in nature-inspired hues also evoke a carefree manner. And cottons even more so; plain or patterned, they do the same.

- Clearly, there isn't much chintz in Parisian flats. Nor are there many bold florals. Stripes, dots, plaids and checks bring pizzazz to relaxed areas, though the look depends upon the scale of the most prominent textile.

In a never-ending quest to lighten mundane tasks, decorative artist Gillian Bradshaw Smith gussied up a laundry room—with hand-painted bed linens billowing in the wind. Fabric from Sea Cloth. Wall covering by Carlton V.

PRECEDING OVERLEAF: *What better place to prepare dinner than in a summer kitchen before moving to a loggia overlooking the pool. Unless, of course, one prefers dining alfresco at a café table; the coolest tables are forty-two inches tall.*

❧ Authentically French, monochromatic toiles de Jouy (pronounced twälz-da-'zhwee) grace furniture, lamp shades, and walls. Story-telling rural and mythological etched scenes—printed in sepia, red, violet, aubergine or indigo on the finest cotton ground—originated in the eighteenth-century Oberkampf factory in the town of Jouy-en-Josas, near Versailles.

❧ Color-drenched cotton prints called *indiennes*—first produced in seventeenth-century India and then imported to France—look right at home in Provence, among the lavender and painted pieces—where the lifestyle is casual. In Parisian circles, seldom are they seen.

❧ The eighteenth-century European rage for chinoiserie in all its many varieties remains *en vogue* to this day. The curved shapes of fish, birds, flowers and pagodas offset harsh lines.

❧ Whether adorning the skirt of a sofa, an ottoman or a chair, deep bullion fringe softens tailored lines while dressing up a room.

❧ Without looking as if it is trying, fringe mitigates hard edges on throw pillows while camouflaging seams and zippers, which are hardly chic.

❧ Alternatively, nail head detailing sends a more rigid signal, especially when profiling leather-clad club chairs. In a dispatch to the design world, Coco Chanel outlined a sofa with nail heads in the twenties, forever ensuring their popularity.

❧ The humble sit across from the grand, the ordinary across from the extraordinary, not necessarily talking points. Easily overlooked accessories perceived as poor relations of their more refined neighbors help signal that good taste is not about personal wealth or visual extravagance.

In 1879, the Swiss chocolatier Rodolphe Lindt developed a special technique using generous quantities of cocoa butter while prolonging the mixing period. "Conching," as the method became known, revolutionized the chocolate industry. By 1899, Lindt had become a brand name.

It is no small feat to be organized, but even in a mudroom order can affect the human spirit positively.

🐦 Mellow wood pieces with warm, varied patinas ground a room with light walls while simultaneously promoting the perception that a setting has evolved over time.

🐦 Two wood pieces sitting side by side gives rise to the sense that something is amiss. Fabric separating wood finishes can erase any hint of a rivalry.

🐦 Most important, finishes need space to breathe, with sturdy silhouettes requiring ample negative air space. Only then can texture influence the character of a room in a positive way.

In a decidedly feminine bedroom, an Étamine fabric embroidered in France unfurls over a classic canopy bed skirted in Cowtan & Tout, at once creating the feeling of a big-girl room for a special young girl and guaranteeing the furnishings will work forever. The sprawling embroidered monogram by Joan Cecil adds a dramatic, dreamy dash.

New or old, a desk is a necessity in any bedroom, even if at times it is prone to lend itself to daydreaming. Here, glass knobs from Anthropologie enhance the vintage look, while embroidered linens from Designers Guild make a fashion statement.

UPPER LEFT: For centuries the armoire has been the quintessential French Country furnishing. It seems safe to say, however, that none match the one shown here, thanks to Shaun Christopher Designs, Dallas, who turned a lifeless one into one that's vibrant. The blanket rack, painted a pretty pink, seemingly holds what every well-dressed little girl playing big girl will be wearing this season.

LEFT: A chandelier from Jan Showers, Dallas, brims with petal power, boosting the room's sparkle.

OPPOSITE: Open, an armoire serves as an "entertainment center," brimming with spots for books and other treasures, including a mirrored jewelry box from Hip Hip Hooray, Dallas, which, of course, is indispensable in a girly room. The Cowtan & Tout rainbow stripe prevents shelves from snagging precious belongings.

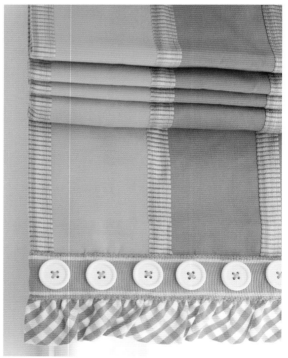

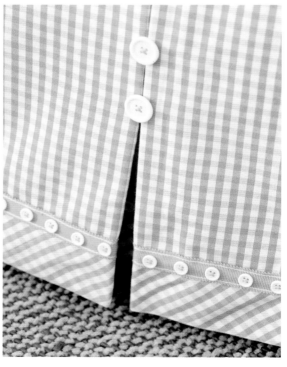

Never one to sit still for long, Emily springs from the best-selling children's book **Emily Goes Wild** by Betty Lou Phillips, struggles to fit her fashion-forward wardrobe into her own très chic trunk (replete with drawers and hanging space), then checks in to this breathtaking room. The irresistible monkey's penchant for beignets, tutus and mischief——not exactly in this order——has elevated her to celebrity status with help from Kids Preferred. To find Emily and her swanky belongings, log on to www.kidspreferred.com, or simply have a look at the closest Barnes & Noble or FAO Schwarz in New York.

LEFT: Trust small details to make a big statement. Petite buttons circle the bedskirt while larger ones embellish the Zimmer + Rohde Roman shades. Trimmings are from Samuel & Sons.

Awash in dangling pink baubles, wall covering from Candace Olson Kids dresses up the bathroom as D. Porthault scalloped towels add an even greater splash of color. The heart print was made for the Duchess of Windsor, who patronized the linen purveyor. Smocked shades, lined and interlined, provide privacy.

UPPER RIGHT: *Inside and out, sconce shades——fabricated by Ceil Johnson, Dallas——flaunt Cowtan & Tout fabrics. Buttons add an artsy, whimsical touch.*

RIGHT: *A bedroom is a world unto itself——a world with spots for sleeping, playing and reading, on a Summer Hill chaise upholstered in Osborne & Little fabric. The antique porcelain stove was unearthed at The Mews, an upscale flea market in Dallas.*

A special place in the heart for nature's splendor led to the creation of a nursery celebrating that beauty, mixing Scalamandré and Winhall fabrics and more. The bed is from LaLune & Company, Minneapolis, while the hickory-branch chandelier——fashioned from naturally felled trees——is by Deanna Wish, New Castle, Pennsylvania; she also crafted the imaginative lamps and then dressed the shades playfully. Far from the commonplace changing table, a rabbit's cage merges function and fun. And who better to keep watch than wise owls, from their own nesting places?

Next to the proper tools, a gardener's best friend is the Department of Agriculture's climate zone indicator on the back of a seed packet.

OPPOSITE: Not all shower curtains are created equal—and not all poems are equally well received. The origin of "What are little boys made of . . ." can be traced to English poet Robert Southey (1774–1843), who also wrote the children's classic The Story of the Three Bears. But since the meaning of "snips and snails" is open to interpretation, we took a little creative license, changing the tale's wording to frogs and snails in keeping with the Scalamandré wall covering. Extra-wide terry cloth is from Rogers & Goffigon.

Outfitted in prestigious Yves Delorme linens, the "Heirloom Poster Crib"——black iron topped with polished brass finials from Benicia Foundry, Benicia, California——is set to cradle a growing baby boy. An abbreviated crib skirt——reflecting a trend——floats above an area rug from Stark Carpet that is sufficiently soft to crawl on.

OPPOSITE: *Nowadays, size matters when it comes to closet space. Plenty of floor space will soon accommodate everything from tractors to trucks, meeting the young occupant's needs and inclinations as his personality evolves. Then baskets from Pottery Barn Kids will also get extra points for holding puzzles and other paraphernalia.*

Reflecting the art of French living, soothing shades of blue and green and inviting fabrics welcome guests to luxe accommodations, where a bed from Murray's Iron Works is the focal point and the quiet beauty of fresh flowers and watercolors by Daniel Heath are fitting complements.

Even the most discriminating guests are likely to be charmed by the sophisticated series of watercolors by Daniel Heath (1985–). Raised in a family with design sensibility, drawing has been his strongest passion from an early age, nurtured by his mother's interest in interiors and his maternal grandfather's architectural accomplishments. The latter, Jack Wood (1921–), taught him how to refine his drawing skills, and then introduced Daniel to painting, which he called "a release from the constraining lines of architecture." Following a family vacation to Paris, eleven-year-old Daniel began to draw from the photographs his parents took, and his appreciation of classical architecture grew. He is a recent graduate of Auburn University, a modernist architectural school.

LEFT: As if taking its cue from Empress Josephine Bonaparte, who was said to have taken extraordinary care over the smallest detail, the Cameron Collection's Drexel chair has a tight rolled back, contrasting bows and a skirt outlined in flange—resembling a ruffle that isn't gathered. Together they add up to comfort that sets the chair apart.

OPPOSITE: While other rooms in the house may hold onto the spirit of the Old World, icy green Brunschwig & Fils wall covering and Waterworks mosaics reflect new-world thinking. Helping set a serene tone: Cowtan & Tout fabric and Samuel & Sons trim on the tub window.

"A well-spent day brings
happy sleep."
—Leonardo da Vinci

A mix of new and vintage frames filled with family photos makes an impressive photo album, while a pier mirror goes to great lengths to offer all the amenities a houseguest could possibly need.

UPPER LEFT: A chair and bar cart stocked with ice and bottled water welcome guests, adding another bit of luxury to a plush retreat.

LEFT: How chocolate came to be left as a nighttime treat in fine hotels worldwide, is anyone's guess. But reportedly, when the Spanish princess Maria Theresa became engaged to the French king Louis XIV in 1643 she hoped to win his heart with a gift of chocolate. And though his many mistresses proved more tempting, she claimed that the king and chocolate were her only passions. No matter, chocolates left on fresh, turned-down sheets can help make a guest's stay an overnight success.

OPPOSITE: A steel bed and desk from Michael Shannon & Associates, San Francisco, put a French forties spin on a guest room's country look. Dramatic chocolate brown walls (Benjamin Moore HC 76 Davenport Tan) enhance the profile of Pierre Frey's sumptuous white matelasse bedecking curtains and bed coverings. White Egyptian cotton linens with two lines embroidered in brown are from the Hotel Collection of Frette, Italy's luxury bedding supplier to homes and fine hotels worldwide.

A gold rush: edgy "Night Life" from Edelman Leather slithers across a wood frame to create a message board.

OPPOSITE: *Haute style and high functionality meld seamlessly, making the most of an unassuming space by turning it into a chic office. The Venetian glass chandelier, lustrous gold sheers fabricated by Design Services, Dallas, and David Easton's fashion-forward "Rococo Leopard" wall covering can't help becoming focal points anymore than creating a feeling of grandeur. The framed black-and-white hand-painted tiles are by Ruben Toledo, a modern-day Ludwig Bemelmans, author of the famous Madeline books. But rather than focusing on "twelve little girls in two straight lines," Toledo's art spotlights fashion, which is only natural since his wife Isabel designs fashionable clothes.*

With a sense of drama and thanks to an artist's eye, a powder room resembles the projection room of an AMC theater.

No trip to a home theater is complete without a stop in the lobby at the concession stand. This one offers more than popcorn and the usual fare.

OPPOSITE: Looks can be deceiving. Indeed, most would never guess that what appears to be fabric covering this theater door is not what it seems. Instead, it is trompe l'oeil, a delightful deception designed to fool the eye.

Le
Salon

LE SALON

Le salon par excellence is, indeed, a work of art, awash in France's storied culture and splendid architecture. Often, however, it is a setting's tangible links to caring ancestors who lived centuries before that spark awe, making the most abiding impression.

Unlike family castoffs that dwell in American homes only until we can afford to replace them, the French savor the pleasure and prestige of furnishings that come their way, thinking of themselves as stewards of the past entrusted with pieces of history that are fit to reign forever in the most coveted spots.

But, then, who could begrudge an armoire—the celebrated source of Gallic pride—such regal treatment? Built in the thirteenth century for storing armor, the armoire has risen to iconic status since becoming emblematic of French country life. Variations abound, so comparisons are inevitable, of course. And certainly some do stand well above the fray. Most prized of all are those with deep carving, shaped bonnets and the patina of age—the distinctive luster resulting from centuries of exposure to heat, humidity and light, to say nothing of oil from loving hands, being that the first thing people often do is touch a piece of furniture.

Yet, the consensus is that looks are not everything. Whether modest or magnificent, the point of pride confirming value and status is provenance—a document authenticating origin and chronicling previous ownership, including identifying the experts who have vetted the piece in the past. Even an armoire that might not ordinarily merit a second look commands respect when accompanied by a paper trail of its meanderings. But, then, any tale—real or far-fetched—adds immeasurably to the cachet, and readily enhances the worth.

No matter that an armoire may unavoidably overshadow other elements in the room. For centuries, the French have favored large-scale furnishings of noble proportions. And how could it be otherwise? As large *châteaux* throughout France have given rise to smaller *maisons* and less-spacious *appartements*, it stands to reason that furniture would still have the imposing look expected, when the custom of handing down family heirlooms remains unchanged.

Predictably, then, the armoire isn't the only heirloom reestablishing its preeminence. Rock crystal (colorless quartz) chandeliers, *trumeaux* (painted overmantels) and screens with painted scenes offer the reassuring feel of the familiar while bringing drama to spaces. At the same time, densely woven tapestries peering down from walls paint *salons* with further importance.

In those that want for nothing, chairs of different sizes and ages are tell-tale signs that sites have evolved over time. Matching ensembles—namely anything indistinguishable from the next, including five-piece place settings of the same china—hold no interest. Nor, it seems,

do many reproductions of originals, which could mean settling for some key differences.

With insistence on quality inherent in French genes, Gauls are remarkably disciplined—capable of living for years without a rug, tapestry, commode or other object of desire until one that is worth possessing comes along—meaning a piece that is finely crafted, with presence and the patina of age. Or, often, one that reaches back to their childhood. To their way of thinking, it is inexcusable to live in a house full of meaningless pieces with no ties to the past, and even worse, one furnished at a hurried pace with pricey items lacking character. While, admittedly, Americans are often driven by desires rather than needs, the pressure to think twice before infusing a room with furniture is a deterrent ingrained in the French national psyche. Consistent with their Gaullist upbringing, more than necessity must prompt the desire to buy.

In bygone eras, imperial-looking *récamiers*, settees, *bergères* (fully upholstered armchairs with enclosed sides and exposed wood frames) and *fauteuils*

With three rows of drawers, short legs and a shape suggestive of a sarcophagus, or tombeau—the French word for tomb—a Régence (1700–30) commode en tombeau, transported to the U.S. from a Paris flea market (marché aux puces) now nobly welcomes guests. Bronze oil lamps that are antique wear hand-painted sheet metal shades known as tôle.

(upholstered armchairs with open sides) stiffly hugged the perimeter of a room. These days, artfully grouped seating—including ottomans and chaise lounges parked in front of fireplaces—make it easy for a people with appreciation for the decorative arts and a passion for intellectualizing to discuss most anything, including pressing concerns. Ingrained in polite society is an aversion to talking about personal finances or materialistic attachments, however. And never would one ask others what they do for a living.

While some people prefer letting bare *parquet de Versailles* or stone put on their own floor show, others are drawn to the beauty of hand-loomed Orientals. Purists, though, favor time-worn *Savonnerie* area rugs, once woven for royalty, and faded *Aubussons*, with their tapestry-like weave that add an air of dignity.

Yet, with the country's 10 million dogs, or one for every six citizens, clearly having the run of houses, practicality is often a weighty consideration influencing design choices.

Nostalgia aside, durable sisal sprawled across hardwood floors suggests a laissez-faire lifestyle, the thinking goes. Humble jute, coir and sea grass—used for centuries—also epitomize today's easy ways. Not everyone loves natural grass rugs, however. Dozens find the texture too abrasive for bare feet and infants' knees, causing it to lose some of its cachet.

Tailored slipcovers with couture-inspired detailing—piping, corner pleats and flat rather than frilly skirts—aim to protect seating, with luxurious fabrics hidden underneath. For that matter, they also camouflage weary furniture, giving pieces a fresh look far less expensively than replacing or reupholstering tattered textiles. At their intimate best, they fit sofas, chairs, and ottomans perfectly—while adding polish to looks.

Even tightly edited spaces host heroic-sized family portraits and photographs in frames, freshly cut flowers arranged *en masse*, and well-read books heaped high on coffee tables that are roomy enough to hold chess boards. (Noticeably absent are plants.)

Reflecting the French obsession with details: a mailbox.

Shapely side tables that withstand the rigors of playful, ever-present dogs offer places for glasses of France's prestigious wines and plates of the country's endless varieties of cheese. Always there are plump pillows—stitched from vintage textiles—to rest against and supple throws that look equally pretty front and back draped romantically, not by chance.

Bolstered collectively by good taste and their legendary passion for detail, the French have the ability to make decorating appear effortless—an attribute not easy to come by, particularly for a people deliberate in their thinking. And yet, the aim behind their efforts is not immediately apparent.

With Parisian sensibility, bergère chairs flaunt pink linen and the loveseat is a lush mohair stripe, coloring the world.

OPPOSITE: *Setting the stage for an array of classical furnishings and fabrics: a Louis XVI bergère, dating back to 1780, and a Louis XV fauteuil—an upholstered armchair with open sides—circa 1760. The chairs flank a period provincial Louis-Philippe (1830–48) cherry desk that greets one upon entering the living room.*

Stairs lead to the breakfast room and kitchen.

OPPOSITE: *A dining room paneled in a mixture of white and red oak veers from predictable formality——at times becoming a study with a round library table before easily reverting back to a space for entertaining. Then, the pearwood French forties sideboard, quite possibly by Frenchman Jacques Quinet (1918–92), functions as a buffet. The chandelier, inspired by a 1930s Emilio Terry (1890–1969) design, is one of only four made. Although an artistic success, it was considered a commercial failure since it was both difficult to transport and complicated to install.*

A massive cabinet morphs into a center island after holding nineteenth-century architectural drawings.

OPPOSITE: After winning the hearts of those in the restaurant industry, high-style and high-performance stainless steel appliances have without reservations made their way into classic kitchens. In the sixteenth century, the taste for monogrammed table and bed linens spread from royal residences to châteaux, and then hôtels particuliers and pieds-a-tierre. Whether simplistic or elaborate, monograms began as efficient laundry marks——often hand stitched in colorfast red——that made a concerted effort to ensure freshly washed linens were returned to their rightful owners.

A nineteenth-century zinc sign that once welcomed shoppers to a boucherie (butcher's shop) lures visitors to this French Country kitchen. The oil painting is by J. Doizette, circa 1908. Standing on the nineteenth-century Italian chest are Swiss cows carved during the same era.

OPPOSITE: A stately, narrow passage leads from the entry to the kitchen.

A fountain with or without running water readily offers a respite from the often hectic outside world.

OPPOSITE: *Understandably, a loggia that is easily accessible from the breakfast room is a favorite spot for morning coffee as well as gatherings later in the day.*

Well-Dressed Windows

Central to the *salons* that harbor them, billowing window treatments screen unappealing views, guard privacy, filter direct sunlight, and, not least, solicit admiring glances. With or without dangling *passementerie*—trimming and tassels—cascading down leading edges, they hang as glamorously as exquisitely constructed ball gowns, dazzling the eye while revealing the French celebrated fascination with beauty.

Until not so long ago, most every fashionable Parisian apartment with *parquet de Versailles* floors and *portes-fenêtres* (floor-to-ceiling windows) that resemble doors, resounded with grandiose curtains that not only seemed to outweigh some segments of the population but also did more for the fabled textile mills hidden outside Lyon—France's third largest city after Paris and Marseille—than imagined. No more.

In a sign of the times, perhaps, settings appear less opulent lately. Conspicuously missing are elaborate, over-the-top cornices hovering above windows, swags (fabric lengths spilling in front of the glass), and jabots (side pieces framing the pane) that many people nowadays consider the height of pretension and a bit much for rooms with precious little floor space. Even valences—certainly a staple in English country houses—are becoming passé. Like cornices, they have a way of visually lowering ceilings, not to mention making windows appear shorter than they are.

Replacing the exaggerated looks that were once the norm, fabrics plunge from ceiling to floor, exalting simplicity. Yes, some curtains framing towering doors and windows tumble with style from eye-catching gilded poles accompanied by carved finials worthy of the past. But still more descend from iron rods and rings.

Mirror images flanking the fireplace bounce light from the windows back into a living room that abounds with antiques, creating comforting richness. At Versailles, the recently restored Hall of Mirrors boasts 357 mirrors, nearly 60 percent original, dating back to the seventeenth century when architect Jules Hardouin-Mansart designed the hall measuring some 240 feet long, 34 feet wide and 40 feet tall. The pillows are vintage Fortuny. Also Italian is the chandelier found at Tara Shaw Antiques, Houston.

Elegantly monogrammed slipcovers——with tone-on-tone embroidery——bring refined style to the dining room opposite, while making striking conversation pieces. Custom-designed frog closures and buttons are from Ellen Holt, Dallas.

Custom-designed slipper chairs from Goodchild Restoration, Dallas, wear fabric from Great Plains, with Clarence House satin detailing edged in nailheads. Originally nail heads covered upholstery tacks, serving as an alternative to expensive, handmade gimp. Both the carpet and the pillow are Aubusson, the latter a remnant layered with trims complementing the living room's palette. In each of his many residences, Napoléon laid Aubusson rugs, which came from the small village in central France bearing the same name.

With practicality and comfort in mind, high-back chairs slipcovered in natural linen by Travers send an invitation to dine in style at a table from Adele Kerr. (Since synthetics attract dirt and heavy fabrics drape poorly, they aren't good choices for cover-ups.) The versatile array of vintage creamware is from the South of France. The sconces are antique.

A grouping of fashion drawings by designer Michael Faircloth, who dressed First Lady Laura Bush for President George W. Bush's 2001 Inaugural Ball, lines the wall. The mirror reflects a ready-made chair from Anthropologie, re-covered in pink velvet.

Although points of view vary on rod placement, one glance confirms the smartest curtains fall from as close to the ceiling molding as possible, making even small rooms look somewhat grander.

Dressmaker headings run the gamut from pencil pleats whose narrow columns generate fullness, to fancier pleats pinched at the top, to painstakingly smocked headings where stitched latticework creates a pattern. What makes all exceptionally alluring are some essential characteristics:

- To preserve natural light, curtains extend beyond the width of the window twelve to fifteen inches on each side, unfailingly mirroring the scale of the room rather than upsetting its proportions.

- For *très chic* richness, workrooms ceremoniously calculate fabric at two-and-a-half—and more often than not, three—times the distance from one end of the curtain rod to the other, including returns—the space from the face of the rod to the wall. There's no skimping on fabric. What's more, the French readily admit that they are not apt to purchase expensive textiles and then fabricate curtains themselves.

- Light streaming in windows silhouettes the beauty of lace. But when it comes to airy sheers or gauzy fabrics that the French call *voilage*—voile, organdy, muslin, batiste—quadrupling a window's width ensures privacy.

- *Au courant* stripes—which Napoléon loved to tout—make their own fashion statement while luring ceilings into appearing taller than reality.

- Working together, lining and hidden interlining block light, absorb sound, help prevent sun damage and turn a casual window treatment into couture. But an unexpected lining—such as an irresistible plaid taffeta peeking from behind a solid silk or wool—alone, adds surprising splendor.

- Lest one wonder: weights stitched in deep, deep hems insure that curtains drape gracefully and then turn under in soft folds.

- Curtains simply brush the floor or "break" no more than three inches. It seems those that "puddle" on hardwoods invariably create niches for pampered pets to sleep. Regardless, the French scoff at curtains that stop short! > 104

A spa-inspired bathroom boasts pink patent leather wall covering and soft, thick, absorbent Egyptian-cotton towels.

LEFT: *Sometimes new won't do. Not when one has her heart set on an antique iron bed, ringed by pale pink walls and gilded crown molding. Shams from Bella Notte Linens wear a gold lace overlay, as does the table skirt. The fabric-covered cube stools offer seats for friends or a place to simply prop one's feet when reading. A mirror——with antiqued glass, gold strapping and medallions—— offers a place to stash photos, invitations and tickets in a fresh way. Meanwhile, the vintage dress form provides a fun place to preview one's attire.*

Photographs from memorable game days surround paraphernalia that telegraphs the interests of the occupant. Suiting a sports lover are the leather sofa from West Elm and lattice stool from Tucker Robbins, New York, serving as a table. Today's thirst for leather dates back to the 1920s, when Parisian designer Jean-Michel Frank first obtained leather from the revered Hermès for use in making furniture.

OPPOSITE: Inspired by a bookcase found in London, a clean-lined, custom-designed cabinet, generously sized to hold photos and trophies in addition to books, gives this boy's bedroom an industrial lift. The map is old; bed from West Elm.

❧ *Passementerie*—rooted in fashion—rouses interest. Tassels hark back to the time of the ancient Egyptians, when they spared embarrassment by snugly keeping royal robes in place. These days, elegant tiebacks and trims have nothing to do with modesty.

❧ Though not as showy as their fringe cousins, braids and tapes supply artful, finished borders with striking individuality.

❧ Narrow piping running down leading edges and streaming across the floor eliminates the need to justify the cost of tempting trim. In the words of twentieth-century tastemaker Sister Parish, "Curtains must always have an edge or an ending," trumpeting a principle of French design that American designers never tire of repeating.

❧ In French eyes, less-than-perfectly-straight seams, a pattern that fails to match or fringe sewn in a questionable manner is any window treatment's undoing.

❧ Handsome natural shades are in keeping with today's less-is-more look, or a yearning for minimalism.

❧ Dressed up or dressed down, Roman shades block the sun's rays and soften windows where curtains would get in the way or simply look like black holes at night. Those mounted with inside brackets draw attention to impressive molding, while shades mounted outside the casing—as close to the ceiling molding as possible—make a window look larger without obstructing either the light or view.

❧ As if to push a short window to the limit, mounting a Roman shade under the curtains gives the window presence. Once again, the guiding rule seems to be that both should be mounted as close to the ceiling as possible.

❧ Contrary to expectations, balloon shades have suddenly joined the ranks of dated, over-the-top window treatments—seldom welcome anywhere.

Every house needs a quiet spot away from the pressures of the world. Here, a Spanish desk sits on a sisal rug with leather binding.

The Fine Art of Exhibiting Art

With its renowned museums and highly respected art galleries, Paris has long been a paradise for art lovers and accomplished artists. It wasn't until 1850, though, that the first gallery opened. No matter that nineteenth-century Paris was the world capital of art. Struggling artists faced the daunting task of finding venues where they could exhibit their work. The needs of those in the art world spurred France's art schools, better known as *académies*, to hold annual and sometimes semiannual exhibitions, or *salons*.

Among the most esteemed was the government-sponsored, eagerly anticipated Paris *salon*, where artists selected by a jury jostled for recognition on soaring walls stacked high with art. Since capturing visitors' attention virtually assured demand for an artist's work, competition was fierce for coveted eye-level spots.

Reportedly, the jury—or Selection Committee—rejected works by Pierre-Auguste Renoir, Claude Monet, Alfred Sisley, Jean Bazille, Camille Pissarro, Paul Cézanne and Edouard Manet, whose distinctive, revolutionary way of capturing light *en plein air* went against established tastes at the time. To appease them, Napoléon III (1852–70) founded the now-famous *Salon des Refusés* (Salon of the Refused) in 1863, which encouraged the French and others to view the Impressionists with new understanding, shifting public perception, albeit reluctantly—yet, in fact, ultimately bringing them widespread attention.

As it happens, to this day Europeans stack paintings and drawings high on walls and over doors in a manner called *salon* style. Meanwhile, on this side of the Atlantic, works of art loom in a *moderne* fashion—that is, in a single row surrounded by ample space.

Rich mahogany paneling wraps a study with bookshelves spanning three of four corners. Beyond the shapely sofa with pink throws and "frog" chairs designed by Michael Taylor hangs a lithograph by French postimpressionist painter Paul Cezanne (1839–1906). It is printed in black with watercolor additions. The Cameron Collection made the ottoman.

Either way, displaying works of art is an art in itself, much harder than it looks, even for a people seemingly having a sixth sense for style. It is hardly any wonder, then, that the French borrow tips from none other than their famous museums that offer timeless lessons in placing art, any more than that they add a few ideas of their own.

❦ Paintings make a stronger impression when congregated together, hung inches apart rather than scattered around the room.

❦ Some of the strongest groupings mass similar subjects—say, landscapes, ladies, children, fruit, animals, birds, flowers or tightly arranged botanicals or architectural plates—creating a focus of their own. This is not to say an assembly of works must be single-minded to fuse seamlessly; only that a sole subject offers an organizing principle.

❦ Indeed, decking a wall with a thought-provoking composition of oil paintings, watercolors, gouaches and drawings can shape a single arrangement.

❦ Large or small, a work of art that eclipses the rest—in value or in sentiment—is worthy of pride of place at the center of a grouping, readily drawing the attention of those entering the room. The honor is a testament to its significance.

❦ A small painting hung beneath a larger one arouses interest. Naturally, it is best to view some artwork at a distance, other work up close.

❦ Different-sized frames arranged in a rectangle—either horizontal or vertical—creates a sense of order. Balance is achieved from the center out, right and left. (In horizontal groupings with a modern twist, an imaginary line separates two rows: the bottoms of the top row of frames hang in a straight line, and the top of frames in the lower row form a straight line. Generally, between the rows, there is about eight inches of space. In a vertical grouping, the outer edges of frames line up.)

With an air of authority, a confidante—with angled seats facing different directions attached in a single unit—holds court, sumptuously robed in fabric from Beaumont & Fletcher. The area rug from Tajzoy Oriental Rugs, Dallas, was woven in Tabriz, Iran.

Since 3000 BC pewter has been used to make practical objects for the home. Nowadays, Neiman Marcus showcases Match pewter, handmade by northern Italian artisans.

OPPOSITE: *Prized copper pots, striking tile from Ann Sacks and a Dacor commercial range garnish a French-inspired kitchen.*

🦋 Many museums insist on pairing works with frames from the same period. Not that this is an easy thing to do. It is rare to find age-appropriate frames in the flea markets, mostly because not many survived the French Revolution, much less two world wars.

🦋 A frame should never overshadow the art. Then, again, an impressive frame can garner added respect for a less-than-important work of art by giving it a stronger presence.

🦋 For pared-down simplicity, a stretched canvas can hang frameless against a backdrop of dramatic architecture.

🦋 An ancestral portrait need not be by Élisabeth-Louise Vigée-Le Brun (1755–1842), Queen Marie Antoinette's favorite portraitist, to perch on an antique easel. Most any generous painting can offset a tall wood piece across the room or interrupt a line of furniture all the same height.

🦋 The idea of propping paintings on fireplaces reaches back to seventeenth-century England. At the time, lofty gilt mirrors hung above smoke-stained chimneypieces in France's grandiosely paneled rooms, coloring the capital's gray light. Some *boiserie* had oil paintings inset. Paintings also adorned the tall, narrow spaces between windows, as they still do. But these days, works of art often stand on fireplaces, too.

🦋 The French are ever mindful that direct sunlight never falls on prints, watercolors or textiles. Fading, yellowing and foxing can result from overexposure to light; heat can crack oil paintings.

An artfully fashioned tea-washed Bennison floral—from an early document—appears to have aged over time, giving this master bedroom an extra touch of grandeur. Resting at the foot of the Patina bed is a bench from Rose Tarlow for Melrose House.

🦋 Although not all works of art need be illuminated in identical ways, low-voltage picture lights often hang above paintings in France. Meanwhile, lighting has gone high-tech in museums and homes on North American shores.

Their idea of eating out? En plein air. Starting with a cool table and other finds from Pottery Barn Kids, and ending with vanilla ice cream dipped in chocolate.

OPPOSITE: *Stepping up efforts to please with a mix of dreamy fabrics from Cowtan & Tout, fresh, inviting linens and custom bedding by Couch, Ltd., Dallas, cannot help but also flatter the hand-painted Jane Keltner bed. The result: a room that is classic and sweet.*

OVERLEAF: *A pavilion——set apart from the main house——reflects the home's French architecture and offers a dramatic place for entertaining.*

A
Tàble

A TÀBLE

While we find it difficult to curb an appetite for gleaming stainless steel commercial ranges and glass-front refrigerators to complement wine coolers stocked with fine champagne, most all the staples of high-tech performance these days are missing in French kitchens.

Appliances sit in plain sight. There are no honed *pietra cardoza* stone countertops or family-friendly islands touting togetherness, let alone twenty-first-century computer centers lauded for their own prowess.

Noticeably absent, too, are paneled upper cabinet doors. Instead, open shelves brim with pitchers, pottery, glassware, platters, trays and other paraphernalia illustrating just how passionate the French are about their cuisine.

Unlike North Americans, who tend to tuck clutter out of sight in designated cabinets, the French prefer that cutting boards, *porte-couverts* (cutlery holders with knives that carve, chop, pare, peel and dice), richly glazed *confit* pots, small appliances and baskets for storing fresh bread vie for counter space with collections of tin molds—some for baking, some for chocolate making and some to satisfy cravings for sorbet or ice cream. Windowsills meanwhile, flaunt mossy pots of sage, rosemary, chives and basil.

There's no question that French kitchens can rightly boast of being incredibly efficient, with an array of equipment designed to steam, strain, boil and drain within easy reach. Scores of pans, colanders and bowls in every size imaginable crowd *crémaillères* (pot racks), as if letting the world in on the merits of copper—or at least selling the younger generation on the notion.

An eighteenth-century enfilade (with the requisite three or four doors) from Umbria, boasts nineteenth-century apothecary jars—watched over by Georgiana, the much-loved family cat.

PRECEDING OVERLEAF: *Embroidered pillows grace a sofa upholstered in antique thistle cloth—a hemp fabric—while a pair of Venetian mirrors whose original glass dates back to the eighteenth century flank Louis XIV armchairs and a bergère chair dressed in lavender gingham. Chairs are from Houston's Tara Shaw, Ltd., and W. Gardner, Ltd., respectively. An antique Oushak, of Turkish descent, sprawls on the floor.*

Once-lifeless doors take on new vitality after being transported from Italy and hand scraped. Beforehand, one exposed panel clearly hinted that this was a possibility.

Upper Left: *An antique slide bolt now adorns each of three eighteenth-century doors (two unseen).*

Opposite: *In a hall awash in light——that doubles as a space for extra tables when entertaining——sixteenth-century stone walls transported from a mas (farmhouse) in Provence serve as a backdrop for seventeenth-century stone floors from nearby Montpellier, southwest of Avignon. From the same era stems a faience container——ideal for holding an olive tree——produced in Nevers. During the reigns of Louis XIII and Louis XIV, the town was an important center of fine glazed pottery production.*

As if on cue, hardwood floors sweep uninterrupted from dining rooms in some regions. Sleek black-and-white tile lends distinction in others. Far from an afterthought, oversized unglazed squares or octagons of terra-cotta tile have the flavor of Provence, Burgundy and the Loire Valley, where clay is plentiful and there's ample charm.

In a country long the uncontested capital of *haute cuisine*, most kitchens are surprisingly small, thanks to everything from being more about cooking than socializing, to resistance to change from the time when they were servants' domains, to homeowners who perhaps lack significant sums to invest in expanding and improving their kitchens. By comparison, Americans spent a record $228 billion in 2007, up more than $6 billion from 2006, satisfying home-improvement dreams, according to findings from Harvard University's Joint Center for Housing Studies.

A farm table proudly showing its age is surrounded by four benches——together seating eight——slipcovered in lavender linen. The linen napkins, hotel silver and faïence are vintage. Older still is the seventeenth-century branched, three-light lustre candelabrum (chandelier with crystal pendants) from Lombardy. Also Italian is the pair of eighteenth-century wall-mounted sconces, or appliqué in French.

Humble stone stairs that once graced a farmhouse in northern France deliver Gallic charm to a well-stocked wine cellar.

OPPOSITE: When an ordinary tasting room won't do, an Henri Lepind painting dated 1883 can lend even more pizzazz. Unseen is a temperature-controlled wine cellar amply stocked with a well-rounded selection.

With purple no longer the domain of kings, a shapely lavender slipcover freely takes its color cue from across the room.

LEFT: A collection of sixteenth- and seventeenth-century Hispano-Moresque reflejo metálico (Italian earthenware) from the town of Maniffes near Valencia rests on an eighteenth-century console, while a nineteenth-century French landscape painting hovers overhead.

OPPOSITE: Global influences add more than a bit of distinction to a stateside breakfast room where a Louis XIV limestone cheminée, as it is called in France, serves as a focal point nearly four centuries after beginning life in a bastide—a small cottage or villa. Adorning the fireplace is a nineteenth-century English charger, signed Lambeth. Pine planks on the ceiling hail from Sweden, while the reclaimed beams shipped from France. The buffet is Tuscan. All are from Chateau Domingue, Houston, and are fitting testaments to owner Ruth Gay's keen eye and passion for the past.

Le Croissant

Legends claiming the croissant actually originated in Austria abound, though it has long been associated with France. According to the most celebrated, early one morning in 1683, while fashioning decadent creations, Viennese bakers heard strange noises and alerted authorities, who discovered that the Turks were tunneling underneath Vienna—and credited the bakers with saving the city. To the latter, it seemed symbolically fitting that people would enjoy devouring the enemy. So, extracting the crescent from the Turkish flag, the bakers shaped their dough, commemorating the Viennese victory over the Ottoman Turkish Empire. Seemingly, the *Harper Collins Robert French College Dictionary* supports this culinary myth; in French, *croissant* means "crescent"—and in a cross reference, *viennoiserie* is *croissant*.

What's more, even the French concede that nearly a century after the fall of the Ottoman Empire, it was Princess Marie Antoinette—sent from her native Austria to marry the future Louis XVI in 1770—who introduced the *croissant* to France.

Today *boulangeries* sell various kinds of breads, satisfying tastes for both the croissant and the baguette, whose roles in the culture are firmly established. In fact, the price of the latter was regulated by the government until 1987. *Patisseries* sell pastries.

A mix of eighteenth- and nineteenth-century faïence nestles in a narrow pine cupboard embedded in a breakfast room wall. The soaring showcase dates back to the nineteenth century.

Interplaying textures—fabric, wood and stone—fill an informal breakfast area where "marriage sacks" grace chairs. In nineteenth-century France, family names were often stamped on burlap grain sacks—and grain was considered an ideal wedding gift.

OPPOSITE: *Across the way (from the cupboard on the page 131), vintage faïence, hotel silver, glassware and antique baskets line a nineteenth-century linen press. Open shelving offers easy access.*

While some may covet high-tech wizardry, others prefer a kitchen with the look of Provence. Amplifying the allure are European architectural elements from Chateau Domingue, Houston, known nationwide for stocking antique doors, floors, stone and more.

OPPOSITE TOP: A shallow stone sink, formerly used for making goat cheese in a monastery near Avignon, brings seventeenth-century French charm stateside. The cobblestone floor, too, is seventeenth century, amassed from a street in Portugal before laid piece by piece in this kitchen. Provençal yellow pottery is nineteenth century.

OPPOSITE BELOW: Propped among the batterie de cuisine are vintage breadboards that lure us back to the lost art of bread making.

Fine Dining

At candlelight fêtes designed to please the senses as much as the palate, tables overflow with a galaxy of crystal surrounded by striking mixes of heirloom china patterns, oversized linen napkins and well-polished family silver.

By common consent, perhaps, the handle of each piece of sterling silver flatware sits near the table's edge, while the dessert spoon and fork lie above the plate. In keeping with the French mind-set, the dessert spoon rests closest to the plate's rim, with its handle to the right, as if hinting that it may join the other spoons on the right side of the plate. Above the dessert spoon lies the dessert fork, with its handle to the left.

Unlike other cultures, the tines of forks face down, resting on the tablecloth——a custom some say developed to undercut the fork's ability to snag ruffled lace sleeves. Others claim someone thought the tines of forks and bowls of spoons looked less aggressive face down, saying nothing about drawing attention to engraved initials without being obvious. But in fairness, the flip sides liberally borrow flourishes from various chapters of French history and often are even more decorative.

Water and wine goblets meet directly above each plate rather than above the knife and spoon as in the States. A regal "underplate," called a charger by Americans, is integral to the table's beauty; it is removed before the first course is served.

Centerpieces are always low——with fresh flowers straight from the garden or from local markets——so they do not interfere with conversation. Indeed, much is made of an unwritten rule: whether debating the workings of their nation or commonplace issues, discussions must continue after the meal, even after a lingering one followed by dessert. For one to simply pick up and leave without engaging in further conversation is considered an affront, as then a dinner party is thought less than successful.

Certainly terra-cotta tile and reclaimed beams haven't lost their allure. It is only that the market is flooded with options meriting more than a glance. It stands to reason, then, that on this side of the Atlantic we are spending more and more on high-tech kitchens, even if, as reported, we are cooking less and less.

Mosaic tiles on the back stairs are a companion to those in the kitchen.

OPPOSITE: A large dining room feels more intimate, thanks to Shaun Christopher Designs, Dallas, who hand stenciled the walls then gave them gold highlights. The Bergamo fabric on the host and hostess chairs drifts onto the outside backs of the side chairs. The rock crystal chandelier is by Dennis & Leen, chosen for its simplicity.

Detail of the kitchen floor.

Hand stenciling adds a touch of verve to the groin-vaulted ceiling, while glazing gives walls added dash. The Chinese developed the technique of stenciling around 300 BC.

OPPOSITE: Generously sized, hand-forged iron chandeliers——7 feet tall, 5 feet in diameter——designed by Richard Gordon, Dallas, hover overhead, adding character while defining conversation groups. The curtain fabrics are from Jim Thompson and Rose Tarlow. The hand-printed velvet on the lounge chairs is custom from TylerGraphics, New York.

Silver Flair

Worldwide, sterling is 925 parts silver to 75 parts copper, honoring the universally accepted norm established in the fourteenth century. While it is treated with respect here in America, the French are less than enamored with *second standard silver*—a term that refers to the ratio of purity in pieces marked with the numeral two.

Since the eighteenth century, *first standard silver*—composed of 950 parts silver to 50 parts copper and adorned with the numeral one—has been a notable source of French pride while garnering an international roster of admirers intent on passing it down for eternity. Some pieces bear the maker's personal stamp. But the hallmark always reveals the district where crafted, while the control mark bespeaks the year produced.

It was Napoléon who set uniform silver marks throughout France, beginning with the *Coq* (rooster), followed by the *Vieillard* (old man), which gave way to the head of Minerva in 1838.

Now as then, sterling ages gracefully unless called into service only on holidays, while stainless flatware becomes duller with use. And though French flatware is larger than that produced in America, one doesn't feel its heaviness, thanks to its design.

With metallic the new neutral, gold strie walls by David Lyles, Dallas, sets a sophisticated yet relaxed mood. Custom bedding is by Straight Stitch. Hand-painted chinoiserie bed tray is from Rose Tarlow for Melrose House.

Fresh green-and-white gingham from Pindler & Pindler gets a harmonious boost from lavender—as both the walls and the carpet pick up on the purple stitching in the check. Wall-to-wall carpeting is from Interior Resources; bedding and area rug are from Pottery Barn Kids.

Living in grand fashion requires a smart niche to breeze through homework.

OPPOSITE: *What young girl wouldn't want to say good-bye to ho-hum tile? Or invite dazzling bits of jewel-toned cracked glass to rim her bathroom mirrors? Tile is from Antique Floors. Artwork is by Peter Max. Terry-topped vanity stool is by Waterworks.*

Pinehurst No. 2
Hole 8 Par 4
JEFF M   (+8)
1st Shot 465y 14' Downhill

What course to next play? There's no need to consult a travel agency any more than to check the weather or call ahead for a tee time, not when there's an in-house simulator replacing some of the most challenging and well-known courses in the world. Full Swing Golf, Inc., offers ample possibilities, as well as a place to stay, meals and other amenities. Here, knotty-pine walls, distressed and hand stained, give the golf room the feeling of an old-world pub with a twist.

La
Chambre

LA CHAMBRE

Back in the eighteenth century, the bedroom was where high-level meetings took place—until Madame de Pompadour, the most famous of Louis XV's mistresses, removed her chambre from the list of public rooms. Gathering the trappings of an enviable lifestyle around her, she announced that privacy was the ultimate luxury. Then, in a quiet revolution, she boldly sealed her quarters from uninvited glares. Only then did her bedroom become worthy of being called a boudoir, fulfilling its promise as a place to pout or sulk.

When travel is not what it once was, why hunt for your passport or fly off to a luxury hotel when there is nowhere better than these luxury accommodations at home?

PRECEDING OVERLEAF: *Deftly tailored skirts cover bare chair legs, prompting the feel of a divine destination where guests are encouraged to protect their skin from the sun while enjoying the fresh air. And best of all: a beloved pet is welcomed!*

The head-spinning ascension of Jeanne-Antoinette Poisson from modest beginnings as wife of a Parisian tax farmer to irresistible mistress stunned the royal court. But even those detractors who criticized her and called her "fish face" behind her back—since in French *poisson* means fish—recognized her influence over the king and could not resist following her lead. Indeed, the protocol she set in place forever altered Gallic bedroom culture, as all of France mirrored her example.

Nowadays, etiquette dictates that bedroom doors remain shut, both day and night. If not, it is poor manners for a person to peer into another person's *chambre* on the way to, say, the powder room, whether or not someone is in the room. Almost always, the French close the shutters adorning their homes at night, much like Americans might hang a sign on the door requesting "privacy."

No different from the time of the ancient Egyptians, eighteenth-century beds were the ultimate symbols of wealth. As a result, rivalry for matchless levels of splendor fueled an array of variations.

Befitting a majestic mansion, Madame de Pompadour and Louis XV's love swirled in a *lit à la française* (canopied bed)—with a crown presiding overhead. Opulent bed hangings billowed romantically, creating a luxurious room within a room when untied.

To this day, the French lavish extraordinary attention on their beds. Most all sheets are white or ecru and posh Egyptian cotton if not 100 percent linen, which becomes softer and whiter with age. Not hampered by thread count, which Consumer Reports say can be misleading beyond 340 threads per inch, there is awareness of the comfort bedding offers and the amenities of splendor: embroidery, appliqué and applied laces. Those not inclined to compromise their standards covet long, thin, single-ply fibers for extra softness and durability, and pillowcases with an interior flap that not only hides the pillow from view but also helps keep it in place.

Borrowing a glamorous mix of style and drama from eras past, a dressing table may add to the setting's allure. *La table de toilette* actually made its debut late in the eighteenth century. Historians say that Madame de Pompadour ceremoniously encouraged courtiers seeking the king's favor to present themselves at an hour when she would be *à la toilette*. Feeling that she looked especially attractive at that time enticed her to abandon her need for privacy.

These days, a *boudoir* is as likely to serve as a spot for corresponding as for sleeping, so it typically includes a writing table. And, though area rugs often grace spaces, bare floors are common, too. Seldom do the French lay carpet—and it is unheard of for them to purchase a bedroom suite with wood finishes boringly alike. What's more, closets are rare. In fact, some say that armoires owe their enduring esteem to satisfying the need for storage space in rooms.

Proper marigold curtains complement sumptuously scaled Murray's Iron Works furnishings, making an outdoor setting off the great room ideal for entertaining any time of day. Also cool: stylish, water-repellent canvas Perennials fabrics in solids, stripes and patterns that rinse clean after a heavy rain.

With a character all its own and a view to match, an unassuming breakfast room offers the perfect spot for reading the morning paper.

OPPOSITE: *Steeped in old-world charm—patterned wood floors, mosaic tile work and lime-finished cabinetry—a kitchen reinvents itself for the new world. The result? A space that is capable of comforting, surprising and delighting in equal measure.*

No matter that wine bars are one of today's hottest trends, some homeowners prefer hosting more intimate gatherings in their own cellars.

OPPOSITE: *Tasting rooms at wineries have become a big business, drawing millions of people to their facilities. But a wine room in one's home can also exude a hospitable tone.*

A postcard-perfect setting is worthy of a French home.

OPPOSITE: *Whether embracing family or friends, having guests for dinner just became easier, from the look here.*

Bed Culture

While one might think twice about shipping a bed from a Paris flea market, there's no reason not to consider adopting France's artfully layered bed culture when searching for a good night's rest. In a twist on tradition, it goes against the natural order of things, paying the rest of Europe little mind.

Apart from what one sees, a stuffed and quilted mattress pad tops the mattress, followed by two flat sheets, then a blanket covered by another sheet. During the coolest months, a *couette* (comforter) filled with *duvet* (down) that comes from the underbellies of geese (eiderdown fill is ultra light and the priciest) traps the warmth. Come morning, the French fold *les couettes* at the foot of the bed.

In the French mind, a bed is not complete without *un traversin*—a long, firm, round bolster spanning the mattress's width. Often it is wrapped in a blanket cover; always it supports European square pillows. The middle sheet reveals a monogram or the family crest applied so that a person standing at the foot of the bed can read it readily.

Detail of the tailored bedskirt.

OPPOSITE: *Reportedly, Queen Marie Antoinette wrapped not just her boudoir at Versailles in toile but other rooms too, perhaps prompting her husband, Louis XVI, to honor the supplier——the Oberkampf factory in the Paris suburb of Jouy-en-Josas——with the "Citation Royale de Manufacture." Following the American Revolution, toiles traveled to the United States, where designers began mixing the fabric with solids, stripes, checks or small-scale plaids staying within the same colorway. Here, the beige-and-white toile is deliberately this guest room's only pattern, just as it would be in France. Pillows wearing antique lace are from Anichini. The embroidered bed linens are by Frette.*

In an arched niche near the staircase opposite is a French settee with wood inlay, circa 1870. Both the settee and the antique table are from Pittet, Dallas. The original lithograph is signed Paul Lelleu, 1905.

OPPOSITE: An iron staircase with a warm bronze finish is the perfect backdrop for a small Empire table and mahogany commode in the style of Charles X. Charles X was Louis XVI's brother and the last Bourbon king to rule France.

Echoing the tones of the Egyptian rug,
Travers textiles cover both the sofa and chairs,
while the pair of antique Régence footstools
boasts their original damask fabric. Velvet
on pillows dates back to nineteenth-century
Somalia. The black lacquer game table,
mahjong set and chairs once belonged to the
homeowner's grandmother.

Soaring limestone walls and tall metal windows surround a dining table and vintage chairs covered in Edelman leather charmed by light. Plump hydrangeas, or hortensia, as the French call them, fill the container. The French grow dozens of beautiful varieties of these showy, lacey flowers, and those who don't have space to do so can be seen gathering them at the local market on summer mornings.

OPPOSITE: *When it comes to decorating, a great room intended for family often gets less-important furnishings than the living room, but not here. The slender, hand-painted leather panels are eighteenth-century French, as are the blue-and-white Chinese export plates assembled on the wall. The chairs and rug are nineteenth century.*

Pristinely painted cabinets with recessed panels and bead mouldings extend
to the ceiling, flanking the stainless steel Décor range with marble slab
backsplash. Adding Parisian flair: Lagos Azul limestone flooring and
Avanza crushed quartz countertops. The lavender topiaries are compli-
ments of Nicholson-Hardie Garden Center, Dallas.

Getting Personal

Taking a walk back in time, monograms began as efficient laundry marks—often hand stitched in colorfast red—that made a concerted effort to ensure freshly washed linens were returned to their rightful owners. They moved to places of honor in nineteenth-century Victorian hope chests, awaiting impending marriages. But long before then, nuns, who learned the art as children, elegantly hand embroidered ornate lettering on church vestments.

Actually, by the mid-sixteenth century, the taste for monogrammed table and bed linens reached royal residences and then added a layer of respectability to dwellings beyond. Fancy or not, personalized linens were refined extensions of oneself, much like a signature deliberately crafted reinforces a stylish image. For each letter formed part of the next, as if intent on making a lasting impression by remaining forever intertwined.

Still, Diane de Poitiers, mistress of Henri II (1519–59), somehow managed to alter the official monogram of the French king and his queen, Catherine de Medici (1519–89), changing the intertwined H and C to H and D.

Today, monograms no longer are the domain of the rich and noble, of course. But they are regal indulgences adding to the price of beautiful linens. Across Europe, people begin assembling tabletop and bed linens for a baby girl's *trousseau* the moment she is born. Tradition dictates that the first letter of her given name reign on the left and the first letter of her surname on the right. The center awaits the first letter of her future husband's family name.

Antique Limoges china, "Jardin du Paradise," by Theodore Haviland. The stemware is Baccarat; the sterling flatware is Buccellati.

OPPOSITE: *By the eighteenth century, more than a million pieces of blue-and-white hand-painted china had shipped to Europe from China. Inspired by the Chinese color palette and designs, English potters developed a technique of transfer printing, permitting mass production. In turn, Staffordshire became an important center of transferware production.*

A pastry table gleams with antique silver and tempting desserts not unlike those seen at Ladurée, one of Paris's grandest tea salons. Acclaimed since 1862, this grand café offers some of the city's most luscious pastries, including much-lauded macaroons.

OPPOSITE: *A breakfast room flowing from the kitchen retains its own identity.*

An outdoor room with comforts equal to an interior setting reflects the good life, regardless of the time of year.

La Chambre · 179

As accent hues mix in startlingly attractive ways, antiques add interest. The nineteenth-century trumeau is characteristic of the era, with a framed mirror less prominent than the decoration, including a painted scene in the upper section of the carved panel.

Résidences
Secondaires

RÉSIDENCES SECONDAIRES

Surprising critics of France's casual work ethic—which often includes two-hour lunches, not to speak of its soft economy and high tax rates—is that the French own more second homes than any other people.

Americans agree, naturally, that getaways have their merits. But further reflecting the chasm between American and French attitudes, we tend to view vacation homes as overt symbols of wealth—expensive indulgences, pricey or not, often earned through never-ending workweeks and marathon struggles between career and family—while the French see *residences secondaires* as investments in their well-being, giving day-to-day life enhanced meaning.

Of course, with nearly 20 percent of the country's sixty-two million inhabitants crowded in the ever-more-congested Île-de-France and barely one fourth living in houses, it's hardly shocking that many people seek a retreat along a windswept beach or in a *village perdu*, which translates loosely as a rural town in the middle of nowhere or simply away from the proximity of neighbors, as pleasant as they might be.

For years, people fearful of appearing elitist tended to shy away from second-home ownership, given all the talk of restraint, not to mention virulent dislike for suburban sprawl and drawing attention to dissimilar economic means. Helping fuel today's trend is growing acceptance, it seems, that holding court in a spot inherited from a caring aunt, or even in a place that comes at a price, indicates passion for one's homeland and nothing more. That said, in France, vacation homes seldom look like vacation homes stateside, with castoff furnishings, old mattresses, outlet linens, and little art. That they are chic extensions of primary homes is never in question.

Befitting a home inspired by the French seaside town of Ile de Ré—a popular escape for Parisians plus a tourist destination—a nineteenth-century bow-front commode spied at the Paris flea market became the impetus for taking an informal approach to a traditional entry. No matter that the dwelling is far from France's western coast, a nineteenth-century eagle goes considerably further than a nautical mile in creating interest after leaving a prominent French château. Vintage paintings reflected in the mirror pay homage to France's maritime history.

PRECEDING OVERLEAF: *Mirror image sofas dress in Belgian linen in keeping with the getaway's white, cream and taupe tone-on-tone palette. L'Afrique, c'est chic. But in a break with tradition, a playful zebra print brings an unexpected touch of the exotic as an alternative to the French penchant for leopard print. An armoire, the hallmark of any French home, is nineteenth century. Floral sisal sweeps the floor, adding texture to the space and giving it a "green" edge.*

Certainly, looks vary widely from one address to another, taking shape according to one's resources and definition of style. (It could be argued, in fact, that some fall short of American glossy ideals as well as those of *Maison Française*, the leading French shelter magazine.) Rarely, however, do the French stray from their unified approach to decorating, which is faithful to a heritage that has long spurned royal excess. Whether a storied *mas* (farmhouse) outside Provence's ancient walled city of Avignon, a *folie* (gentleman's getaway perfect for romantic rendezvous) along a stretch of Normandy's legendary coastline, or a whitewashed house in the seaside town of Île de Ré, chic, comfortable, welcoming spaces—some less formal than others—do the late monarchs proud.

Delivering laid-back style: a generously sized limestone tabletop supported by nineteenth-century columns. The latter once adorned a South Carolina Antebellum mansion and still wear original paint. An ideal chandelier happened upon at the Paris flea market lends flair. The English cupboard, circa 1860, formerly stored courthouse documents. Layering French ironstone, vintage hotel silver and stemware by Juliska adds to the global look sans formality.

Taking its cue from the French, who serve only the freshest bread and an incredible array of produce, a kitchen offers a visual feast. The iron lantern is from a home in England. Cabinets were stained then sanded back. Hand-scraped floors are quartersawn red oak.

OPPOSITE: *A nineteenth-century trestle table that hails from Belgium works as a desk. It is laden with eighteenth- and nineteenth-century books centered on the French Revolution.*

Fashioning diplomatic ties, distinctive French enamelware known as majolica and tableware made by England's Johnson Bros. suggest a healthy meal is on deck. And though interchangeable patterns generally create a tablescape that's surprising, these, oddly enough, both inspire thoughts of fresh fish at a seaside restaurant where the catch of the day is plated soon after being purchased from a docking boat. Chairs upholstered in environmentally friendly raffia are from Vintage Living, Dallas.

OPPOSITE: Scaffolding salvaged from Belgium gives a coffee table elevated status; oyster sticks were used in constructing its base. Even miles from the ocean and sand, sponge coral gathered in one's travels can bring dash. A geometric sisal defines the seating arrangement.

Les
Details

LES DÉTAILS

In the seventeenth century, Louis XIV and his visionary finance minister, Jean-Baptist Colbert, established a strictly controlled guild system that regulated the work of artisans, raising the specialties at which they excelled to even higher standards.

More than three centuries later, the Sun King's perfectionism remains his extraordinary gift to France, though his penchant for overt opulence may be better known.

While the latter legacy might always endure, King Louis XIV deserves credit for influencing most everything the French do. From their insistence on finely crafted furniture and regal textiles to turning out rooms with dignity and panache, attention to the smallest detail is testimony to the late king's fastidiousness and in keeping with his foresight. Whether selecting quality leather for a chair or replacing door hardware, settings are a matter of careful planning and styling. In fact, the attention to minutiae is striking.

Finely etched knobs, surface bolts, and *crémone bolts* that could almost pass for artwork bestow added nobility on groaning doors and tall, narrow windows. Crisp crown moldings, seamlessly woven, step out onto ceilings, making spaces appear even taller than they actually are. Polished brass grilles with scrolled motifs adorn heating vents, elevating the ordinary. Bullion is deep rather than shallow, giving upholstery a more sophisticated look. The trims embellishing vintage textiles fabricated into throw pillows are full, not skimpy, illustrating that doubling is key to winning acclaim.

Poised between the dining room and living room, an entry's shapely accessories and hand-painted lamp capture visitors' interest while setting the mood of the home's interiors. Offering proof that small touches can make a big difference is a table from Domain XCIV, Fort Worth.

PRECEDING OVERLEAF: *Fabric frames the entrance to a dining room, creating the feel of a country house outside of Paris by lending intimacy and ceremony.*

Whereas small paintings would disappear on generous walls, grouped with mirrors and wall sconces they make a strong statement. Meanwhile, heroic-sized family portraits add splendor and historic character.

Disregarding the American practice of leaving eight to eighteen inches of exposed wood around the perimeter of a room, ample-sized area rugs cross boundary lines, making smaller carpets appear skimpy, and rooms look larger than they are. Even in close quarters the French think big, opting for a few furnishings—always exaggerated in size rather than modestly scaled.

Further suggesting the sophistication of a former era, several rock crystal chandeliers may drift overhead in the same room, while sconces wearing shades wash walls with light, picture lights cast a soft glow and table and floor lamps direct glare. Together they maneuver light into producing drama and warmth not attainable with overhead sources. To be sure, the French often shy away from track lighting, which can jarringly cast unforgiving shadows on the face.

It is not, however, as if any list can claim to be exhaustive. But attention to the smallest detail makes a setting memorable. What's more, it is a shining testament to France's artistic past. For it glorifies the image of the Sun King, whose influence is still felt these hundreds of years later.

Plays of texture——meaning opposites that attract, including rough and smooth——help an entry make a positive first impression. The hand-painted leather tapestries are from the Horchow Collection. Chairs covered in brick red offer a place to catch one's breath.

Playful pigs adopted from TAO Schwarz, New York, wear buttons in their ears—a Steiff trademark. People the world over collect stuffed animals from the company founded in Germany more than a hundred years ago by Margerete Steiff.

RIGHT: Most everyone knows that Emily, Emma, Jacob and Michael have topped the list of favorite names for newborns in recent years. But an unscientific survey suggests that for longer still animals from Old MacDonald's farm have been summoned to make children's bedrooms fun spots to play during the day and comforting places to hit the hay at night. Here, imagery by Dallas artisan Beth Campbell partners with hardworking fabrics, ensuring this space will work well for more than the time being.

Rather than trying to hide a mail slot that would have been difficult to conceal, the designer enhanced its look. Nearby, a diverse group of altar sticks create an ambiance centuries old.

In France, a portrait may hang over the mirror above a commode. But in a never-ending quest stateside to reinterpret the style of the French, another mirror may top the mirror.

OPPOSITE: France's first royal library, the Bibliothèque du Roi, or King's Library, sited in Paris, dates from the reign of Charles V (1364–80).

OVERLEAF: An array of textiles and textures meet in the living room, where a leopard from Travers dashes across the ottoman. The nineteenth-century armoire is walnut.

RESOURCES

ANTIQUE FURNISHINGS AND ACCESSORIES

Agostino Antiques, Ltd.
21 Broad St.
Red Bank, NJ 07701
Telephone 732.345.7301
agostinoantiques.com

Ambiance Antiques
135 Rhode Island St.
San Francisco, CA 94103
Telephone 415.255.9006
ambianceantiques.com

Anthony Antiques & Fine Arts
401 E. 200 S.
Salt Lake City, UT 84111
Telephone 801.328.2231

Area
5600 Kirby Dr.
Houston, TX 77005
Telephone 713.668.1668

Bremermann Designs
3943 Magazine St.
New Orleans, LA 70115
Telephone 504.891.7763
bremermanndesigns.com

Brian Stringer Antiques
2031 W. Alabama St.
Houston, TX 77006
Telephone 713.526.7380
brianstringerantiques.com

Carl Moore Antiques
1610 Bissonnet St.
Houston, TX 77005
Telephone 713.524.2502
carlmooreantiques.com

Charles Gaylord & Co.
Two Henry Adams St., Ste. 406
San Francisco, CA 94103
Telephone 415.861.6300
charlesgaylord.com

Château Domingue
3615-B W. Alabama St.
Houston, TX 77027
Telephone 713.961.3444
chateaudomingue.com

Country French Interiors
1428 Slocum St.
Dallas, TX 75207
Telephone 214.747.4700
countryfrenchinteriors.com

Décor de France
24 N. Blvd. of the Presidents
Sarasota, FL 34236
Telephone 941.388.1599
decordefrance.com

Donald J. Embree Antiques
1115 Slocum St.
Dallas, TX 75207
Telephone 214.760.9141

Duane Antiques
176 Duane St.
New York, NY 10013
Telephone 212.625.8066
duaneantiques.com

East & Orient Company
1123 Slocum St.
Dallas, TX 75207
Telephone 214.741.1191
eastandorient.com

Ed Hardy San Francisco
188 Henry Adams St.
San Francisco, CA 94103
Telephone 415.626.6300
edhardysf.com

The French Hare, Ltd.
418 King St.
Charleston, SC 29403
Telephone 843.577.0451
thefrenchhare.com

The Gables
711 Miami Cr.
Atlanta, GA 30324
Telephone 800.753.3342
thegablesantiques.com

Galerie de France
184-186 Duane St.
New York, NY 10013
Telephone 212.965.0969

Gore Dean Antiques
2828 Pennsylvania Ave.
Washington, DC 20007
Telephone 202.625.1776
goredeanantiques.com

The Gray Door
3465 W. Alabama
Houston, TX 77019
Telephone 713.521.9085

Inessa Stewart Antiques
5330 Bluebonnet Blvd.
Baton Rouge, LA 70809
Telephone 225.368.8600
inessa.com

Inessa Stewart Antiques
5201 W. Lovers Ln.
Dallas, TX 75209
Telephone 214.366.2660
inessa.com

Jacqueline Adams Antiques
2300 Peachtree Rd., Ste. B 110
Atlanta, GA 30309
Telephone 404.355.8123
jacquelineadamsantiques.com

Jacqueline Adams Antiques
The Galleries of Peachtree Hills
425 Peachtree Hills Ave.
Atlanta, GA 30305
Telephone 404.869.6790
jacquelineadamsantiques.com

Jane Moore Interiors
2922 Virginia St.
Houston, TX 77098
Telephone 713.526.6113

Jefferson West Inc.
9310 Jefferson Blvd.
Culver City, CA 90232
Telephone 310.558.3031
jeffersonwest.com

John Rosselli & Associates
523 E. 73rd St.
New York, NY 10021
Telephone 212.772.2137
johnrosselliantiques.com

John Rosselli & Associates
255 E. 72nd St.
New York, NY 10021
Telephone 212.737.2252
johnrosselliantiques.com

Joseph Minton Antiques
1410 Slocum St.
Dallas, TX 75207
Telephone 214.744.3111
mintonantiques.com

Joyce Horn Antiques
1022 Wirt Rd., Ste. 326
Houston, TX 77055
Telephone 713.688.0507
joycehornantiques.com

Kay O' Toole Antiques
1921 Westheimer Rd.
Houston, TX 77098
Telephone 713.523.1921
kayotooleantiques.com

KM Antiques of London
979 3rd Ave., Ste. 1702
New York, NY 10022
Telephone 212.888.7950

Le Louvre French Antiques
1400 Slocum St.
Dallas, TX 75207
Telephone 214.742.2605
lelouvre-antiques.com

Legacy Antiques
1406 Slocum St.
Dallas, TX 75207
Telephone 214.748.4606
legacyantiques.com

The Lotus Collection
445 Jackson St.
San Francisco, CA 94111
Telephone 415.398.8115
ktaylor-lotus.com

Lovers Lane Antique Market
5001 W. Lovers Ln.
Dallas, TX 75209
Telephone 214.351.5656
loverslaneantiques.com

M. Naeve Antiques
1928 Bissonnet St.
Houston, TX 77005
Telephone 713.524.0990

Maison Felice
73-960 El Paseo
Palm Desert, CA 92260
Telephone 760.862.0021
maisonfelice.com

Mariette Himes Gomez
506 E. 74th St.
New York, NY 10021
Telephone 212.288.6856
gomezassociates.com

Marston Luce
1651 Wisconsin Ave., N.W.
Washington, DC 20007
Telephone 202.333.6800

The McNally Company Antiques
6033 L&M Paseo Delicias
Rancho Santa Fe, CA 92067
Telephone 858.756.1922

Metropolitan Artifacts, Inc.
Architectural Antiques
4783 Peachtree Rd.
Atlanta, GA 30341
Telephone 770.986.0007
metropolitanartifacts.com

The Mews
1708 Market Center Blvd.
Dallas, TX 75207
Telephone 214.748.9070
themews.net

Neal & Co.
4502 Greenbriar St.
Houston, TX 77005
Telephone 713.942.9800

Newell Art Galleries, Inc.
425 E. 53rd St.
New York, NY 10022
Telephone 212.758.1970
newel.com

Niall Smith
306 E. 61st St.
New York, NY 10021
Telephone 212.750.3985

Nick Brock Antiques
2909 N. Henderson St.
Dallas, TX 75206
Telephone 214.828.0624

Parc Monceau, Ltd.
425 Peachtree Hills Ave., # 15
Atlanta, GA 30305
Telephone 404.467.8107
parcmonceauatl.com

Parkhouse Antiques
114 Parkhouse St.
Dallas, TX 75207
Telephone 214.741.1199

Patina Atelier Antiques
3364 Sacramento St.
San Francisco, CA 94118
Telephone 415.409.2299

Pied-A-Terre
7645 Girard Ave.
La Jolla, CA 92037
Telephone 858.456.4433

Pittet & Co.
1215 Slocum St.
Dallas, TX 75207
Telephone 214.748.8999
pittet.com

R.F. Imports
5950 Berkshire Ln., Ste. 1500
Dallas, TX 75225
Telephone 214.696.0152

Round Trip Imports
33071 W. 83rd St.
De Soto, KS 66018
Telephone 913.583.1511
roundtripimports.com

Shabby Slip
3522 Magazine St.
New Orleans, LA 70115
Telephone 504.897.5477

Sidney Lerer
420 Richmond Ave.
Point Pleasant Beach, NJ 08741
Telephone 732.899.8949

Skelton St. John
2143 Westheimer Rd.
Houston, TX 77098
Telephone 713.524.1990

South of Market
345 Peachtree Hills Ave.
Atlanta, GA 30305
Telephone 404.995.9399
southofmarket.biz

RESOURCES

St. Gertrude Antiques
3424 Magazine St.
New Orleans, LA 70015
Telephone 504.897.9258
stgertrude.com

The Stalls
116 Bennett St.
Atlanta, GA 30309
Telephone 404.352.4430
thestalls.com

Studio Veneto
7427 Girard Ave.
La Jolla, CA 92037

Tara Shaw Antiques
1845-A W. Alabama
Houston, TX 77098
Telephone 713.533.9744

Therien & Co.
716. N. La Cienega Blvd.
Los Angeles, CA 90069
Telephone 310.657.4615
411 Vermont St.
San Francisco, CA 94103
Telephone 415.956.8850
therien.com

Tres Belle
2435 East Coast Hwy.
Corona Del Mar, CA 92625
Telephone 949.723.0022

Uncommon Market, Inc.
2701-2707 Fairmount St.
Dallas, TX 75201
Telephone 214.871.2775

Vieux Carré
546 Hudson St.
New York, NY 10014
Telephone 212.647.7633

W. Gardner, Ltd.
2930 Ferndale
Houston, TX 77098
Telephone 713.521.1027
wgardnerltd.com

Watkins Culver
2308 Bissonnet St.
Houston, TX 77005
Telephone 713.529.0597

The Whimsey Shoppe Slocum
1444 Oak Lawn Ave.
Dallas, TX 75207
Telephone 214.745.1800

ARTISANS

Allan Rodewald
Expressive Design Studios
1402 Dart St.
Houston, TX 77007
Telephone 713.988.5570
Allanrodewald.com

Brad Oldham, Inc.
1551 Edison St.
Dallas, TX 75207
Telephone 214.239.3993
bradoldham.com

Chuck Walter
511 S. Elm St.
Arlington, TX 76010
Telephone 817.229.9453

David Lyles
514 Summit Dr.
Richardson, TX 75081
Telephone 972.240.0051
seedavidlyles.com

EyeCon Studios
1341 Plowman
Dallas, TX 75203
Telephone 214.941.0500
eye-c.com

Gillian Bradshaw Smith
311 N. Winnetka Ave.
Dallas, TX 75208
Telephone 214.948.8472

Irene de Watteville
749 N. Granados Ave.
Solana Beach, CA 92075
Telephone 858.755.0627

Jackie Musso
6530 St. Moritz
Dallas, TX 75214
Telephone 214.828.1249

Jennifer Chapman Designs
7049 Via Cabana
Carlsbad, CA 92009
Telephone 760.602.0079
jenniferchapmandesign.com

Jo Mattison
4100 San Carlos St.
Dallas, TX 75205
Telephone 214.521.9337

Joanna Otte Studios
6358 Waverly Way
Fort Worth, TX 76116
Telephone 817.235.8233

Kay Fox's Custom Creations
2404 Springpark Way
Richardson, TX 75082
Telephone 972.437.4227

Patrick Edwards
3815 Utah St.
San Diego, CA 92104
Telephone 619.298.0864

Shaun Christopher Designs
6593 Garlinghouse Lane
Dallas, TX 75252
Telephone 214.597.9059
shaun-christopher.com

BATH FITTINGS

Czech & Speake
350 11th St.
Hoboken, NJ 07030
Telephone 800.632.4165
homeportfolio.com

Herbeau Creations of America
2725 Davis Blvd.
Naples, FL 34104
Telephone 800.547.1608
herbeau.com

Kallista, Inc.
2446 Verna Ct.
San Leandro, CA 94577
Telephone 888.4.Kallista
kallistainc.com

Sherle Wagner, International
300 E. 62nd St.
New York, NY 10022
Telephone 212.758.3300
sherlewagner.com

Sunrise Specialty
930 98th Ave.
Oakland, CA 94603
Telephone 510.729.7277
sunrisespecialty.com

Waterworks
60 Backus Ave.
Danbury, CT 06810
Telephone 800.899.6757
waterworks.com

CARPETS

Abrash Rugs
1025 N. Stemmons Frwy., Ste. 760
Dallas, TX 75207
Telephone 214.573.6262
abrashrugs.com

Asmara, Inc.
88 Black Falcon Ave.
Boston, MA 02210
Telephone 800.451.7240
asmarainc.com

Beauvais Carpets
201 E. 57th St.
New York, NY 10022
Telephone 212.688.2265
beauvaiscarpets.com

Carol Piper Rugs, Inc.
1809 W. Gray St.
Houston, TX 77019
Telephone 713.524.2442
carolpiperrugs.com

Design Materials
241 S. 55th St.
Kansas City, KA 66106
Telephone 913.342.9796

Farzin Rugs & Design
955 Slocum St.
Dallas, TX 75207
Telephone 214.747.1511

Hokanson
Decorative Ctr.
5120 Woodway Rd.
Houston, TX 77056
Telephone 800.243.7771
hokansoncarpet.com

Mansour
8600 Melrose Ave.
Los Angeles, CA 90069
Telephone 310.652.9999

Mark, Inc.
323 Railroad Ave.
Greenwich, CT 06830
Telephone 203.861.0110
brunschwig.com

Nouri & Sons Antique Oriental Rugs
3845 Dunlavy St.
Houston, TX 77006
Telephone 713.523.6626
nouriantiquerugs.com

Renaissance Collection
1532 Hi Line Dr.
Dallas, TX 75207
Telephone 214.698.1000
rencollection.com

Rosecore Carpet Co., Inc.
D&D Building
979 Third Ave.
New York, NY 10022
Telephone 212.421.7272
rosecore.com

Stark Carpet
D&D Building
979 Third Ave.
New York, NY 10022
Telephone 212.752.9000
starkcarpet.com

Stephen Miller Gallery
800 Santa Cruz Ave.
Menlo Park, CA 94025
Telephone 650.327.5040
stephenmillergallery.com

DECORATIVE HARDWARE

E. R. Butler & Co., Inc.
Maison J. Vervloeot-Faces
75 Spring St., 5th Fl.
New York, NY 10012
Telephone 212.925.3565
erbutler.com

Nanz Custom Hardware
20 Vandam St.
New York, NY 10013
Telephone 212.367.7000
nanz.com

P. E. Guerin, Inc.
21-23 Jane St.
New York, NY 10014
Telephone 212.243.5270
peguerin.com

Palmer Designs
7875 Convoy Ct.
San Diego, CA 92111
Telephone 858.576.1350
palmer-design.com

FABRICS & FURNITURE

Anna French
108 Shakespeare Rd.
London, SE 0QW
Telephone 020.7737.6555
annafrench.co.uk

B. Berger Fabrics
1380 Highland Rd.
Macedonia, OH 44056
Telephone 330.425.3838
bberger.com

Beacon Hill
225 Foxboro Blvd.
Foxboro, MA 02035
Telephone 800.343.1470
beaconhilldesign.com

Bennison Fabrics, Inc.
76 Greene St.
New York, NY 10012
Telephone 212.941.1212
bennisonfabrics.com

Bergamo Fabrics, Inc.
D&D Building
979 Third Ave., 17th Fl.
New York, NY 10022
Telephone 212.888.3333
bergamofabrics.com

Boussac Fadini
15 E. 32nd St., 6th Fl.
New York, NY 10016
Telephone 212.213.3099

Brentano Inc.
1451 Paddock Dr.
Northbrook, IL 60062
Telephone 800.338.7210
brentanofabrics.com

Brunschwig & Fils, Inc.
75 Virginia Rd.
North White Plains, NY 10603
Telephone 914.684.5800
brunschwig.com

RESOURCES

The Budji Collections, Inc.
7302 E. Helm Dr., Ste. 2002
Scottsdale, AZ 85260-3126
Telephone 480.905.3126
budji.com

C. J. Dellatore
133 W. 25th St., Ste. 9W
New York, NY 10001
Telephone 212.352.0160

The Cameron Collection
150 Dallas Design Center
1025 N. Stemmons Frwy.
Dallas, TX 75207
Telephone 214.744.1544

Carlton V, Ltd.
D&D Building
979 Third Ave., 15th Fl.
New York, NY 10022
Telephone 212.355.4525

Charles Pollock Reproductions, Inc.
6824 Lexington Ave.
Los Angeles, CA 90038
Telephone 323.962.0440
charlespollockrepro.com

Christopher Norman, Inc.
41 W. 25th St., 10th Floor
New York, NY 10010
Telephone 212.647.0303
christophernorman.com

Christopher Hyland, Inc.
979 3rd Ave., Ste. 1710
New York, NY 10022
Telephone 212.688.6121
christopherhyland.com

Clarence House, Inc.
211 E. 58th St.
New York, NY 10022
Telephone 800.221.4704
clarencehouse.com

Classic Revivals, Inc.
One Design Center Pl., Ste. 534
Boston, MA 02210
Telephone 617.574.9030

Coraggio Textiles
1750 132nd Ave., N.E.
Bellevue, WA 98005
Telephone 425.462.0035
coraggio.com

Cowtan & Tout
111 Eighth Ave., Ste. 930
New York, NY 10011
Telephone 212.647.6900

Delany & Long, Ltd.
41 Chestnut St.
Greenwich, CT 06830
Telephone 203.532.0010
delanyandlong.com

Dennis & Leen
8734 Melrose Ave.
Los Angeles, CA 90069
Telephone 310.652.0855

Donghia, Inc.
256 Washington St.
Mount Vernon, NY 10553
Telephone 914.662.2377
donghia.com

Elizabeth Dow, Ltd.
155 Sixth Ave., 4th Fl.
New York, NY 10013
Telephone 212.219.8822
edowltd.aol.com

Erika Brunson
15442 Ventura Blvd., Ste. 200
Sherman Oaks, CA 91403
Telephone 818.252.4947
erikabrunson.com

F. Schumacher Company
79 Madison Ave., 14th Fl.
New York, NY 10016
Telephone 212.213.7900
fschumacher.com

The Farmhouse Collection, Inc.
807 Russet St.
Twin Falls, ID 83301
Telephone 208.736.8700
farmhousecollection.com

The Florio Collection
8815 Dorrington Ave.
West Hollywood, CA 90048
Telephone 310.273.8003
floriocollection.com

Fortuny, Inc.
D&D Building
979 Third Ave., 16th Fl.
New York, NY 10022
Telephone 212.753.7153
fortuny.com

Gregorius/ Pineo
653 N. La Cienega Blvd.
Los Angeles, CA 90069
Telephone 310.659.0588

Hamilton, Inc.
8417 Melrose Pl.
Los Angeles, CA 90069
Telephone 323.655.9193

Henry Calvin Fabrics
2046 Lars Way
Medford, OR 97501
Telephone 541.732.1996
Telephone 888.732.1996 (toll-free)
henrycalvin.com

Hinson & Company
2735 Jackson Ave.
Long Island City, NY 11101
Telephone 718.482.1100

Indulge Maison Decor
2903 Saint St.
Houston, TX 77027
713.888.0181
indulgedecor.com

J. Robert Scott
500 N. Oak St.
Inglewood, CA 90302
Telephone 310.680.4300
jrobertscott.com

Jan Barboglio
145 Cole Ave.
Dallas, TX 75207
Telephone 214.698.1920

Jane Keltner
94 Cumberland Blvd.
Memphis, TN 38112
Telephone 800.487.8033
janekeltner.com

Jane Shelton
205 Catchings Ave.
Indianola, MS 38751
Telephone 800.530.7259
janeshelton.com

Jim Thompson
1694 Chantilly Dr.
Atlanta, GA 30324
Telephone 800.262.0336
jimthompson.com

Koplavitch & Zimmer Textiles
18600 Crenshaw Blvd.
Torrance, CA 90504
Telephone 866.447.5100
koplavitchandzimmer.com

Kravet Fabrics, Inc.
225 Central Ave. S.
Bethpage, NY 11714
Telephone 516.293.2000
kravet.com

La Lune Collection
930 E. Burleigh St.
Milwaukee, WI 53212
Telephone 414.263.5300
lalunecollection.com

Lee Jofa
225 Central Ave. So.
Bethpage, NY 11714
Telephone 888.LeeJofa
leejofa.com

Malabar Fabrics
8A Trowbridge Dr.
Bethel, CT 06801
Telephone 877.625.2227
malabar.co.uk

Manuel Canovas
111 Eighth Ave., Ste. 930
New York, NY 10011
Telephone 212.647.6900
manuelcanovas.com

Marvic Textiles, Ltd.
30-10 41st Ave., 2nd Fl.
Long Island City, NY 11101
Telephone 718.472.9715
marvictextiles.co.uk

Michael Shannon Associates
722 Steiner St.
San Francisco, CA 94117
Telephone 415.563.2727
s-j.com

Michael Taylor Designs
1500 Seventeenth St.
San Francisco, CA 94107
Telephone 415.558.9940
michaeltaylordesigns.com

Minton Spidell, Inc.
8467 Steller Dr.
Culver City, CA 90232
Telephone 310.836.0403

Mokum Textiles
98 Barcom Ave.
Rushcutters Bay NSW 2011
Telephone 1800 123 705
mokumtextiles.com

Murray's Iron Works
1801 E. 50th St.
Los Angeles, CA 90058
Telephone 323.521.1100
murraysiw.com

Nancy Corzine
256 W. Ivy Ave.
Inglewood, CA 90302
Telephone 310.672.6775

Niermann Weeks
Fine Arts Building
232 E. 59th St.
New York, NY 10022
Telephone 212.319.7979
niermannweeks.com

Nobilis, Inc.
57-A Industrial Rd.
Berkeley Heights, NJ 07922
Telephone 800.464.6670
nobilis.fr

Old Timber Table Company
908 Dragon St.
Dallas, TX 75207
Telephone 214.761.1882
oldtimbertable.com

Old World Weavers
D&D Building
979 Third Ave., 10th Fl.
New York, NY 10022
Telephone 212.355.7186
old-world-weavers.com

Osborne & Little
90 Commerce Rd.
Stamford, CT 06902
Telephone 203.359.1500
osborneandlittle.com

Palecek
The New York Design Center
200 Lexington Ave., Ste. 511
New York, NY 10016
Telephone 212.287.0063
palecek.com

Patina, Inc.
351 Peachtree Hills Ave., N.E.
Atlanta, GA 30304
Telephone 800.635.4365
patinainc.com

Perennials Outdoor Fabrics
140 Regal Row
Dallas, TX 75247
Telephone 214.638.4162
perennialsfabrics.com

Peter Fasano, Ltd.
964 S. Main St.
Great Barrington, MA 01230
Telephone 413.528.6872

Pierre Frey, Ltd.
12 E. 32nd St.
New York, NY 10016
Telephone 212.213.3099

Pindler & Pindler, Inc.
11910 Poindexter Ave.
Moorpark, CA 93021
Telephone 805.531.9090
pindler.com

Pizitz Home & Cottage
121 Central Square
Seaside, FL 32459
Telephone 850.231.2240

Pollack & Associates
150 Varick St.
New York, NY 10013
Telephone 212.627.7766
pollackassociates.com

Prima Seta Silks/Jagtar & Co
3073 N. California St.
Burbank, CA 91505
Telephone 818.729.9333

Quadrille Wallpapers &
Fabrics, Inc.
50 Dey Street, Building One
Jersey City, NJ 07306
Telephone 201.792.5959

RESOURCES

Randolph & Hein, Inc.
2222 Palou Ave.
San Francisco, CA 94124
Telephone 800.844.9922
raldolphhein.com

Raoul Textiles
8687 Melrose Ave., Ste. G-160
West Hollywood, CA 90069
Telephone 310.657.4931

Reynière Workshop
142 Oak Rd.
Monroe, NY 10950
Telephone 845.774.1541

Robert Allen Fabrics
55 Cabot Blvd.
Mansfield, MA 02048
Telephone 800.240.8189
robertallendesign.com

Roger Arlington, Inc.
30-10 41st Ave., Ste. 2R
Long Island City, NY 11101
Telephone 718.729.5554

Rogers & Goffigon, Ltd.
41 Chestnut St., Ste. 3
Greenwich, CT 06830
Telephone 203.532.8068

Rose Cumming Fabrics
Fine Arts Building
232 E. 59th St., 5th Fl.
New York, NY 10022
Telephone 212.758.0844
rosecumming.com

Rose Tarlow Textiles
8454 Melrose Pl.
Los Angeles, CA 90069
Telephone 323.653.2122
rosetarlow.com

Scalamandré
300 Trade Zone Dr.
Ronkonkoma, NY 11779
Telephone 800.932.4361
scalamandre.com

Scully & Scully
504 Park Ave.
New York, NY 10022
Telephone 212.755.2590
scullyandscully.com

Sea Cloth
107 Greenwich Ave.
Greenwich, CT 06830
Telephone 203.422.6150
seacloth.com

The Silk Trading Co.
360 S. La Brea Ave.
Los Angeles, CA 90036
Telephone 323.954.9280
silktrading.com

Smith & Watson
200 Lexington Ave., Ste. 801
New York, NY 10016
Telephone 212.686.6444
smith-watson.com

Stroheim & Romann, Inc.
30-30 47th Ave.
New York, NY 11101
Telephone 718.706.7000
stroheim.com

Summer Hill, Ltd
2682 Middlefield Rd.
Redwood City, CA 94063
Telephone 650.363.2600
summerhill.com

Travers & Company
504 E. 74th St.
New York, NY 10021
Telephone 212.772.2778
traversinc.com

Zimmer + Rohde
15 Commerce Rd.
Stamford, CT 06902
Telephone 203.327.1400
zimmer-rohde.com

GARDEN ORNAMENTS

Archiped Classis
315 Cole St.
Dallas, TX 75207
Telephone 214.748.7437
archipedclassics.com

Barbara Israel Garden Antiques
296 Mount Holly Rd.
Katonah, NY 10536
Telephone 212.744.6281
By Appointment Only
bi-gardenantiques.com

Elizabeth Street Garden & Gallery
1172 Second Ave.
New York, NY 10021
Telephone 212.644.6969

Lexington Gardens
1011 Lexington Ave.
New York, NY 10021
Telephone 212.861.4390

Tancredi & Morgan
7174 Carmel Valley Rd.
Carmel Valley, CA 93923
831.625.4477

Treillage, Ltd.
418 E. 75th St.
New York, NY 10021
Telephone 212.535.2288
treillageonline.com

IRON WORK

Brun Metal Crafts, Inc.
2791 Industrial Ln.
Bloomfield, CO 80020
Telephone 303.466.2513

Cole Smith, FAIA and ASID
Smith, Ekblad & Associates
2719 Laclede St.
Dallas, TX 75204
Telephone 214.871.0305

Ironies
2222 Fifth St.
Berkeley, CA 94710
Telephone 510.644.2100
ironies.com

Murray's Iron Work
1801 E. 50th St.
Los Angeles, CA 90058
Telephone 323.521.1100
murraysiw.com

Potter Art Metal
4500 N. Central Expwy.
Dallas, TX 75206
Telephone 214.821.1419
potterartmetal.com

LINENS

Casa Del Bianco
866 Lexington Ave.
New York, NY 10021
Telephone 212.249.9224

Casa di Lino
4026 Oak Lawn Ave.
Dallas, TX 75219
Telephone 214.252.0404

D. Porthault, Inc.
18 E. 69th St.
New York, NY 10021
Telephone 212.688.1660
d-porthault.com

E. Braun & Co.
717 Madison Ave.
New York, NY 10021
Telephone 212.838.0650
ebraunandco.com

Frette
799 Madison Ave.
New York, NY 10021
Telephone 212.988.5221
frette.com

Indulge Maison Decor
2903 Saint St.
Houston, TX 77027
713.888.0181
indulgedecor.com

Léron Linens
804 Madison Ave.
New York, NY 10021
Telephone 800.954.6369
leron.com

Pratesi
829 Madison Ave.
New York, NY 10021
Telephone 212.288.2315
pratesi.com

Sharyn Blond Linens
2708 W. 53rd St.
Fairway, KS 66208
Telephone 913.362.4420
sharynblondlinens.com

Yves Delorme
1725 Broadway Ave.
Charlottesville, VA 22902
Telephone 800.322.3911
yvesdelorme.com

LIGHTING, LAMPS, AND CUSTOM LAMP SHADES

Ann Morris Antiques
239 E. 60th St.
New York, NY 10022
Telephone 212.755.3308

Bella Shades/Bella Copia
255 Kansas St.
San Francisco, CA 94103
Telephone 415.255.0452

Brown
2940 Ferndale St.
Houston, TX 77098
Telephone 713.522.2151
theshopbybrown.com

Cele Johnson Custom Lamps
1410 Dragon St.
Dallas, TX 75207
Telephone 214.651.1645

Chandelier
7466 A Girard Ave.
La Jolla, CA 92037
Telephone 858.454.9450

Paul Ferrante, Inc.
8464 Melrose Pl.
Los Angeles, CA 90069
Telephone 323.653.4142
paulferrante.com

Marvin Alexander, Inc.
315 E. 62nd St., 2nd Fl.
New York, NY 10021
Telephone 212.838.2320

Murray's Iron Work
1801 E. 50th St.
Los Angeles, CA 90058
Telephone 323.521.1100
murraysiw.com

Nesle Inc.
38-15 30th St.
Long Island City, NY 11101
Telephone 212.755.0515
nesleinc.com

Niermann Weeks
Fine Arts Building
232 E. 59th St., 1st Fl.
New York, NY 10022
Telephone 212.319.7979
niermannweeks.com

Panache
719 N. La Cienega Blvd.
Los Angeles, CA 90069
Telephone 310.652.5050

Thomas Grant Chandeliers, Inc.
1804 Hi Line Dr.
Dallas, TX 75207
Telephone 214.651.1937

Vaughan Designs, Inc.
979 Third Ave., Ste. 1511
New York, NY 10022
Telephone 212.319.7070
vaughandesigns.com

STONE AND TILE

Ann Sacks Tile & Stone Inc.
8120 N.E. 33rd Dr.
Portland, OR 97211
Telephone 800.278.8453
annsacks.com

Architectural Design Resources
2808 Richmond Ave., Ste. E
Houston, TX 77098
Telephone 713.877.8366
adrhouston.com

Country Floors
15 E. 16th St.
New York, NY 10003
Telephone 212.627.8300
countryfloors.com

M.A. Tile & Stone Design
2120 Las Palmas Dr., Ste. H
Carlsbad, CA 92011
Telephone 760.268.0811

Paris Ceramics
151 Greenwich Ave.
Greenwich, CT 06830
Telephone 888.845.3487
parisceramics.com

RESOURCES

Renaissance Tile & Bath
349 Peachtree Hills Ave., N.E.
Atlanta, GA 30305
Telephone 800.275.1822
renaissancetileandbath.com

Roof Tile & Slate Company
1209 Carroll St.
Carrollton, TX 75006
Telephone 972.242.7785
claytile.com

Tesserae Mosaic Studio, Inc.
1111 N. Jupiter Rd., Ste. 108A
Plano, TX 75074
Telephone 972.578.9006
tesseraemosaicstudio.com

Unique Stone Imports
1130 W. Morena Blvd.
San Diego, CA 92110
Telephone 619.275.8300
uniquestoneimports-sd.com

Walker Zanger, Inc.
8901 Bradley Ave.
Sun Valley, CA 91352
Telephone 877.611.0199
walkerzanger.com

TRIMMINGS AND PASSEMENTERIE

Ellen S. Holt, Inc.
1013 Slocum St.
Dallas, TX 75207
Telephone 214.741.1804
ellensholt.com

Houlès USA Inc.
8584 Melrose Ave.
Los Angeles, CA 90069
Telephone 310.652.6171
houles.com

Kenneth Meyer Company
325 Vermont St.
San Francisco, CA 94103
Telephone 415.861.0118

Le Potager
108 W. Brookdale Pl.
Fullerton, CA 92832
Telephone 714.680.8864

Leslie Hannon Custom Trimmings
665 Vetter Ln.
Arroyo Grande, CA 93420
Telephone 805.489.8400
lesliehannontrims.com

Renaissance Ribbons
PO Box 699
Oregon House, CA 95961
Telephone 530.692.0842
renaissanceribbons.com

Samuel & Sons
983 Third Ave.
New York, NY 10022
Telephone 212.704.8000
samuelandsons.com

Tassels & Trims
232 E. 59th St.
New York, NY 10022
Telephone 212.754.6000

West Coast Trimming Corp.
7100 Wilson Ave.
Los Angeles, CA 90001
Telephone 323.587.0701

DIRECTORY OF DESIGNERS

Laura Lee Clark Falconer, ASID
Laura Lee Clark Interior Design, Inc.
3303 Lee Parkway, Suite 415
Dallas, TX 75219
Telephone 214.265.7272
lauraleeclark.com

Sydney Fiedler
Sydney Fiedler Design
3006 Woodside Street, Suite 7017
Dallas, TX 75204
Telephone 214.468.8338

Dale Gillman
Francie Faudree Gillman
Antique Warehouse
2406 East 12th Street
Tulsa, OK 74104
Telephone 918.592.2900

Richard A. Gordon,
Allied Member ASID
Marilyn Rolnick Design Associates, Inc.
2501 Oak Lawn Avenue, Suite 810
Dallas, TX 75219
Telephone 214.528.4488
marilynRolickDesign.com

Sarah Lander Hast
Lander Mercantile
114 Sunview Street
Sunnyvale, TX 75182
Telephone 972.226.2701

Bill Hendrix
Bill Hendrix Interiors
3521 Oak Lawn Avenue, Suite 121
Dallas, TX 75219
Telephone 817.832.2543

Betty Lou Phillips, ASID
Andrea Smith
Interiors by BLP
4278 Bordeaux Avenue
Dallas, TX 75205
Telephone 214.599.0191
Bettylouphillips@bettylouphillips.com

Pam Pierce
Pierce Designs
2422 Bartlett Street, Suite H
Houston, TX 77098
Telephone 713.961.7540

Carol Ray and Marlene Weitman
Ray-Weitman Designs
6126 Rex Drive
Dallas, TX 75230
Telephone 972.365.0200
Telephone 214.649.1406
rayweitmandesigns.com

Lisa Luby Ryan
Vintage Living
6701 Snider Plaza
Dallas, TX 75205
Telephone 214.360.4211
lisalubyryan.com

Liz Lank Williamson, ASID
Katie Lang
Liz Lank Interiors
6904 North Ridge Drive
Dallas, TX 75214
Telephone 214.460.0367

DIRECTORY OF ARCHITECTS

Larry Boerder, A.I.A.
Larry E. Boerder Architects
4514 Cole Avenue, Suite 101
Dallas, TX 75205
Telephone 214. 559.2285
larryboerder.com

Ken Schaumburg, A.I.A.
Schaumburg Architects
817 W. Daggett Avenue
Fort Worth, TX 76104
Telephone 817.336.7077
schaumburgarchitects.com

Elby Martin
Elby S. Martin & Associates, Inc.
6750 Hillcrest Plaza Drive, Suite 219
Dallas, TX 75230
Telephone 972.991.3529
elbymartin.com

Clint Pearson, A.I.A.
Symmetry Architects
5401 North Central Expressway, Suite 325
Dallas, TX 75205
Telephone 214.691.9119
symmetryarchitects.com

DESIGNER PHOTOGRAPHIC CREDITS

ARCHITECT PHOTOGRAPHIC CREDITS